SOLDIERING UNDER OCCUPATION

Soldiering under Occupation

Processes of Numbing among Israeli Soldiers in the Al-Aqsa Intifada

Erella Grassiani

berghahn
NEW YORK · OXFORD
www.berghahnbooks.com

Published in 2013 by
Berghahn Books
www.berghahnbooks.com

© 2013 Erella Grassiani

Library of Congress Cataloging-in-Publication Data

Grassiani, Erella.
Soldiering under occupation : process of numbing among Israeli
soldiers in the Al-Aqsa Intifada / Erella Grassiani. -- 1st ed.
   p. cm.
Includes bibliographical references.
ISBN 978-0-85745-956-5 (hbk.: alk. paper) -- ISBN 978-0-85745-957-
2 (ebook)
   1. Al-Aqsa Intifada, 2000---Atrocities. 2. Soldiers--Israel--Social
conditions. 3. Soldiers--Israel--Moral conditions. 4. Soldiers--Israel--
Attitudes. 5. Apathy. 6. Military ethics--Israel. 7. Military government-
-Israel. 8. Human rights--Israel. 9. Human rights--West Bank. 10.
Human rights--Gaza strip. I. Title.
   DS119.765.G72 2013

                                         956.9405'4--dc232012032897

British Library Cataloguing in Publication Data

A catalogue record for this book is available from the British Library
Printed in the United States on acid-free paper

ISBN 978-0-85745-956-5 (hardback)
ISBN 978-0-85745-956-5 (paperback)
ISBN 978-1-78238-228-7 (institutional ebook)
ISBN 978-1-78238-229-4 (retail ebook)

CONTENTS

For my mother, Cora Zoutewelle

List of Figures

Acknowledgements

This work could not have been written without the help and support of many. I won't be able to thank you all, but I'll give it a try.

First of all I would like to thank the Netherlands Defense Academy (NLDA) and the Executive Board of the VU University for making this research possible by contributing financially. I also thank the two anonymous reviewers who helped me revise the book to its current state.

I would then like to thank my academic teachers; starting with the late Donna Winslow who introduced me to the world of anthropology of things military. Furthermore, I want to thank Jan Abbink for his supervision and Desiree Verweij for introducing me to the NLDA and for believing in this anthropological adventure into the morality of Israeli soldiers. In particular I want to thank Eyal Ben-Ari, for his encouraging support and for his ability to let me believe in myself, over and over again. Eyal: *Toda!*

Without the great atmosphere of the Department of Social and Cultural Anthropology of the VU University my time there would not have been the same. I want to thank everyone for making me feel at home. In addition I want to mention some special people: Bram for his never-ending enthusiasm and Tijo for not taking me too seriously. During the last stretch of finalizing this book my 'writing club' mates Ellen Bal and Lorraine Nencel were my always-available supporters who encouraged me and convinced me I was on the right track.

I can, furthermore, not forget to thank the 'guys'; the young Israeli men who took the time to relate their sometimes difficult experience of serving as soldiers in the Occupied Palestinian Territories to me. Without their stories there would not have been a book to write. I do hope, however, that in the future their children will have other, more peaceful stories to tell.

A very special thank you goes to Breaking the Silence and Yehuda Shaul in particular for generously giving me access to their testimonies and photo material.

Finally, I would like to thank my 'home base': my sister Ayellet and my mother Cora who were my biggest supporters. Rob who helped with the draft. My father Shmulik, savta Reni and all my other friends and family in the Netherlands, Israel and elsewhere who are too numerous to mention by name: thank you and *toda* for just being there and helping me through the rough patches. Lastly, Adnan, who literally ran into my life, you made finalizing this work so much easier with your endless support and encouragement, *choukran motek.*

PREFACE

In July 2008, the media in Israel and abroad reported about an Israeli infantry soldier who had shot a bound Palestinian arrestee in the foot. This incident was filmed by a Palestinian girl living in the village where the incident took place. This, being a crystal clear example of immoral and illegal behaviour (according to Israeli and international law) on the part of the soldier, triggered military officials to quickly condemn the incident and to state that 'this serious incident negates army values', while Minister of Defence Ehud Barak said that 'this is an unusual and unacceptable incident and it doesn't represent the IDF (Israeli Defence Forces) or its values', after which he added that, 'warriors do not behave like this'.[1]

In April 2012 an IDF officer was filmed beating a Danish protester with the butt of his rifle. The film clip was publicized on YouTube and soon enough the same kind of reactions could be heard from Israeli officials; the incident was condemned and the officer was demoted from his function hours after the story was made public. The message was that this was not IDF-like behaviour.

These two incidents, which are only few amongst many of such events, triggered the same kinds of reactions especially concerning questions of responsibility. In all official discourse the events were denounced and efforts were made to emphasize that the military would take these events seriously. In the first case it would try either the soldier who fired the shot or his commander who the soldier said had given him an order to shoot the bound man.[2] In the second event the officer was refused promotion and was demoted from his current function. Importantly, responsibility was placed with the individual soldier or officer and not with the military system itself.

Such incidents and especially the discourse surrounding them are not only very disturbing, they are also very informative examples of one of the points I want to bring home with this work. As is so often the case, the Israeli military and political establishment chose to look solely at the incident as something detached from its wider context; they tried to present

---

1. http://www.haaretz.com/hasen/spages/1004040.html as accessed on 24 July 2008.
2. Both the officer and the soldier were charged with 'unworthy conduct'. The officer was not reassigned to another post; see www.haaretz.com/hasen/spages/1009176.html as accessed on 18 August 2008. The officer in the second event was demoted 'on moral grounds', see www.nytimes.com/2012/04/19/world/middleeast/israeli-officer-who-struck-protester-is-dismissed.html as accessed on 27 April 2012.

the suspects as 'rotten apples' whose behaviour was despicable and from whom they distanced themselves.[3] They did not take a more structural perspective, one that would incorporate a more complete picture of Israeli soldiers as an occupying force within the OPT (Occupied Palestinian Territories) and the implications such work has on their (moral) behaviour.

This work was born out of a discontent with the official discourses around events such as those described above. The establishment and the military refuse to take any responsibility for the misbehaviour of their officers and soldiers and hide themselves in a cloak of innocence. I am convinced that the system within which these people work is not just an innocent context, but a deeply forming one. Here I want to investigate the processes at hand. What happens when soldiers serve as occupiers within an occupied territory? What factors are of influence on their behaviour, on their moral decision making and on the violence that they use.

This work is then an investigation into young Israeli men and their experiences as soldiers in the IDF while serving in the OPT as combatants. The research is focused on the moral orientation of these soldiers in the context of their everyday lives as conscripts in this particular setting. We could call this work an investigation of micro-ethics, to apply a term Ignatieff (2001) used to indicate the need for research on moral issues in the military at the level of the soldiers and young commanders themselves.

In order to make real sense of the behaviour that Israeli soldiers display when dealing with Palestinian civilians, we need to reach a deeper understanding of the multi-level processes that are at play. I believe it is essential to ask critical questions about what socio-cultural and psychological processes are at play when Israeli soldiers behave in a violent, indifferent or disrespectful manner towards Palestinians and how these processes influence the way the soldiers perceive this situation themselves. As I mentioned before, I think it is essential to look further than the simple perception that such soldiers are just immoral exceptions. We should look deeper into these processes on several different levels in order to find out how such behaviour comes into being on a larger, structural scale, taking into account the kind of conditions within which these soldiers serve.

In this work I will show the way the physical surroundings of the work arenas of Israeli soldiers and their implications have a 'numbing effect' on these soldiers on three different levels: the emotional, the physical and the cognitive. Together with operational dynamics such as routine and power, which I will discuss in detail, these processes of numbing have a great influencing power on the work of Israeli soldiers, their use of violence and their moral competence, which I call a process of moral numbing.

---

3. See also an op-ed about this incident by Manekin, www.ynet.co.il/articles/0,7340,zL- 3571292,00.html as accessed on 20 May 2011.

Methodology

Methods of research are our tools for studying reality. It is, then, important to make clear how the researcher perceives this reality. The epistemological stance within this project is an interpretive one. The researcher and the social world are perceived to influence one another and are not thought of as independent entities. The focus will then be on meanings and interpretations of the informants. The methods that come with such a stance are qualitative in nature. These methods are not only meant to predict, but also to understand results on a deeper level.

Fieldwork for this research was carried out in separate periods between March 2005 and August 2007. During this fieldwork interviews were conducted, trips were made to the Occupied Palestinian Territories and military installations were visited in order to observe the situation on the ground.

Data Collection

To outline the 'emic' discourse used by soldiers when speaking about their experiences in the field, semi-structured and unstructured interviews were conducted with Israeli men who, during their obligatory draft period, had served in combat units that had been active in the Occupied Palestinian Territories during the Second Intifada. By the time of the research, these soldiers numbered in the tens of thousands, making for a large pool of potential informants. Some of the interviewees served as officers and quite a large section served as (junior) commanders. They came from several units that were defined by the IDF as combat units, included different ranks and had performed different kinds of activities during their service. Consequently, the research setting was not one particular geographically bounded setting such as a village, a city neighbourhood or a commercial enterprise, as in most anthropological works.

Besides the interviews, complete testimonies and over a hundred 'descriptions of incidents' collected by the organization Breaking the Silence were made available to me in an unedited form.[4] These valuable texts were analyzed in the same way as the interviews in order to identify central themes and the issues soldiers found important while keeping in mind the differences between both data collections.

Multiple trips were made to the Occupied Palestinian Territories (West Bank) in order to get a realistic view of the soldiers in the setting of their daily work. These trips were more observational than participant: due to military restrictions on outsiders and civilians it is impossible to

---

4. Breaking the Silence is an organization of Israeli ex-combatants that collects the testimonies of soldiers who have served within the OPT; see www.breakingthesilence.org.il. Testimonies collected by this organization are coded as 'BS'.

linger extensively at checkpoints or military installations. During these trips I crossed many checkpoints of different shapes and sizes, I walked through Palestinian cities, I occasionally had a chance to talk to the local population and I drove through the Palestinian landscape for many hours. Furthermore, I witnessed several demonstrations by Palestinians and Israeli activists against the occupation and the appropriation of Palestinian lands. The observations gained from these visits were very important for learning more about soldiers' behaviour, especially when compared to what soldiers said about their experiences – they give an extra dimension to what one has been told. In the case of discrepancies between behaviour and what was said, the question can be raised of why soldiers' statements do not reflect their practice. These discrepancies were not perceived as untruthful but, rather, as very insightful. The observations were also important to 'get a feel' for the landscape, the smells, noises and the weather Israeli soldiers experience while working in the OPT.

Even though participant observation is an anthropological method of the first order, in this project it necessarily occupied a somewhat marginal place, as participating in the daily life of soldiers on duty was not feasible. The military in any country is usually a closed system that is hard for researchers to get into. The Israeli military is no different. As Ben-Ari, Maman and Rozenhek (2000: 95) state: '[T]he IDF combines relative closure to research by external scholars with a number of internal arms that carry out research and only rarely release or publish their findings in publicly accessible forms'. The decision to interview recently discharged soldiers who had served within the Occupied Palestinian Territories after the beginning of the Second Intifada made for a huge pool of potential informants. This method is a proven one, often used by Israeli researchers on military issues (see, for example, Lomsky-Feder 1998; Lieblich 1989; Helman 1993; Ben-Ari 1998).

Reflections on the Role of the Researcher

As 'the social role of the participant observer and the images which respondents have of him [sic] have a decisive influence on the character of the data collected' (Vidich as quoted in Monaghan 2000: 4), it is important to take a reflective stance to see in what ways the researcher's identity or perceived identity influences her research. This is unavoidable and should therefore not be bypassed; an acknowledgement of this fact should be taken into consideration. A few identity traits of the researcher and their effects will be discussed here.

The first issue is doing research within an all-male setting as a woman. Because I did not use the classical methods of participatory observation, it was not necessary for me to 'go native' and live with my research group in one and the same space. This would also have been hard to accomplish, as my informants were not connected to each other in any way other than their military experiences and all came from different military units. The all-male setting was, then, not a geographically bounded one.

Although being a woman who has not served in the military, I am an Israeli citizen, a fact that made the research in many respects easier. First of all, the young interviewees were glad to be able to speak in their native tongue about their experiences. This was obviously easier for them than speaking in English. Furthermore, their often-used military jargon would have been difficult to translate. Additionally, as an Israeli I belonged to their immediate national in-group, as opposed to, for example, foreign journalists and tourists. I shared a common national culture with them that, for instance, made it possible for them to refer to popular TV programmes or famous national figures.

As an academic, however, I was immediately categorized as a 'leftist' on the political scale and this, at times, influenced the answers given and was once even given as a reason for agreeing to be interviewed. The informant in question agreed to speak to me, because he saw it as his task to defend the Israeli military against the negative reports coming from the foreign press; talking to me would be an opportunity to 'show it's not that bad'. Being an Israeli, doing research on such a topic as I was, meant that there was no escaping political opinions. However, as mentioned before, during the research and the interviews I tried to put myself in a neutral position as much as was realistically possible.

Chapter 1

Introduction
Understanding Israeli Soldiers

In this work I argue for a broader, more extensive look into all factors that can influence the often violent behaviour of Israeli soldiers and their moral decision making. Looking at this issue from the point of view of the soldier, I want to gain a deeper understanding into the ways these young men view and interpret their day-to-day lives. I will argue in this work that the behaviour of soldiers under occupation, while performing the work and duties that are implied in the strategies and modes of power employed by the Israeli state and its military, is deeply influenced by the spaces they work in; their work arenas. These work arenas and the spaces they occupy, such as the many checkpoints soldiers man but also patrols and arrests, are the direct physical consequences of Israeli policy in the Occupied Palestinian Territories (OPT). The characteristics of these spaces (such as the way a checkpoint is built or a patrol is carried out) and their operational dynamics on the behaviour of the soldiers and the way they reproduce space, control it and imagine it, I will furthermore argue, result in different processes of numbing. On a physical, emotional and cognitive level, soldiers face a numbing effect that in turn leads to a state of moral numbing. In this work I will elaborate on these arenas, on the operational dynamics that influence the soldiers' behaviour, processes of numbing and on the different discursive strategies they construct to deal with the moral situations they face, whether these are recognized as such or not.

Through its approach and subject, my study fills a gap left open by several different disciplines dealing with the issue of soldiers' behaviour. While much work has been done on the different circumstantial factors that can have an effect on the behaviour of soldiers, little has been written about how the actual space soldiers move and work within can affect their behaviour, especially its moral component. Scholars have looked at the types of conflict soldiers are part of (Ron 2003), types of power that states employ (Gordon 2008) and specific aspects of military organization that soldiers find themselves in (Ben-Ari et al. 2010; Levy 2008). And while space has been connected to the use of power and power relations (Lefebvre 2007), there is surprisingly little material that connects space to the (moral) behaviour of soldiers in the field.

Important work on (urban) space and its use by the military has for example been done by Graham (2004) and Gregory (2004). They both have, amongst other conflicts, looked at the militarization of space in Israel/Palestine. While their work is very insightful and gives us insights on a macro level of the workings of the military and especially the devastation it can bring to urban space, it gives little information on how space that is used, controlled and (temporarily) inhabited influences soldiers and the way they behave and make moral decisions.

This work will fill this gap between the works on situational aspects of the work of soldiers and work on (military) space. It will take a bottom-up approach to unravel the ways soldiers view their day-to-day experiences in the OPT and the way they give meaning to these experiences and meetings with the 'other'; the Palestinian. It will, furthermore, focus on the way soldiers make moral sense of their surroundings and of the activities they perform.

My main argument is then twofold; first of all I will show with my work that the spatial surroundings of soldiers in the OPT deeply influence the moral behaviour of Israeli soldiers and that this spatial influence, with its operational dynamics, enhances a process of numbing on the three different levels mentioned above: physical, emotional and cognitive, which in turn have a profound influence on the moral numbing of soldiers. This moral numbing makes the soldiers unaware of the morally problematic aspects of the situation they find themselves in and can lead to an increased use of violence and harassing behaviour.

Second, I argue that within this space Israeli soldiers construct specific moralities through different (verbal) strategies of legitimization and denial of their actions when telling about them. These used strategies 'help' soldiers to cope with their experiences and explain them to themselves and outsiders, while often avoiding responsibility.

Here I want to stress that the overall contribution I hope to make with this work can be found on several different levels. This work stands at the meeting point of several different disciplines, contributing to knowledge within these disciplines and, in turn, using their concepts as part of the analytical framework. This book, first of all, is part of the growing corpus of social research on violence and the military. It contributes, however, to a neglected topic: the morality of soldiers within the area of their daily activities. Here the anthropological character of the work is important, it looks at these abstract terms from a bottom-up approach, giving voice to the actors, soldiers in this case, involved.

Second, this research contributes to the small niche represented by the anthropology of moralities. While much anthropological work has been done on the values and norms of different societies, research aimed at uncovering the moralities of specific groups of people has been limited (with exceptions such as Howell 1997 and Zigon 2008).

Third, the discipline of military ethics shares a similar research subject to that of this project: looking at the moral decision making of military personnel. However, within military ethics the researcher often looks at the situation that is to be analyzed from above, in terms of how soldiers should behave and what rules and codes should be designed for them. In contrast, this work aims to look at soldiers themselves and at the setting they work in every day in order to see how their reality looks in moral terms.

On a fourth level, this work will try to make a social contribution. Understanding the violent behaviour of soldiers will, hopefully, help to avoid such confrontations in the future, not only by contributing to solutions to curb harmful and humiliating confrontations between military personnel and civilians by emphasizing the contributing factors of such behaviour, but also by encouraging others to take a more systemic view of the conflicts soldiers are sent to and the situations they are put in. By understanding the effects of the practices of occupation on the behaviour of soldiers, one should also pose questions regarding the legitimacy of certain conflicts and/or occupations and the way they are conducted.

In order to establish such a deep understanding into the experiences of soldiers it is important to understand the social and historical context in which they were brought up and to identify what social and cultural baggage they take with them when they arrive in the Occupied Palestinian Territories to perform their compulsory military service. Furthermore, some background information is needed on the conflict that these soldiers are part of and the way I conceptualize it.

Israel: a Militarized Society

Zionist thought imagined an ideal 'New Jew': a native born who was strong, handsome and most of all, a good fighter that was to be the antithesis of the ghetto and/or diaspora Jew (Wistrich 1995, Ohana 1995, Shohat 1990). This Zionist ideal and its military counterpart, in many ways, can still be detected in Israeli society today. When thinking about a 'militarized society', one might think of an intimidating military power that spreads fear in the streets of a country. However, one could say the opposite is the case in Israel, where the sheer comfort and familiarity of its society with the military presence characterizes its militarism. Of course this only goes for the military within Israeli society, not its role and influence within Palestinian society.

To this day, Israel practises compulsory conscription; men are called up for three years, women for eighteen months. All Palestinians living within Israel except for the Druze community are exempted from this conscription. A small minority of Bedouins volunteer to serve in the IDF, often as trackers. Jewish Orthodox men who are students at a *yeshiva* (religious school) are exempted under the Tal Law, which is very controversial in Israel; Orthodox and married women are also exempted from military service.

We can safely say that Israel is home to a militarized society in the sense of soldiers and army commanders being omnipresent and strongly influential in the public sphere, within which an idealization of the fighting soldier is still evident. Furthermore, this military presence and these ways of thinking are accepted and 'naturalized' because they are seen as necessary and inevitable in conditions of structural insecurity. The military, its material (i.e. military vehicles, army bases and symbols) and human representatives as well as its influence in the political and economic realm, can be found everywhere in Israeli society. Kimmerling called the kind of militarism present in Israel a cognitive militarism (1993). By this he meant 'modes of thought and action in which security considerations are pre-eminent' (Lomsky-Feder and Ben-Ari 1999: 6). In the way people look at the world in such a society and in their way of thinking, things military are normalized and become an accepted part of life.

Military service for Jewish Israelis was for a long time perceived as an almost natural 'rite de passage' for Israelis (see, for example, Lieblich and Perlow 1988; Dar and Kimhi 2001), a phase during which one gives to the nation in order to get back its services and protection. In Levy's words this is a materialist militarism by which he means that the power bequeathed by military service can be converted into good positions and material benefits in civilian life (Levy 2003). When costs outweigh the benefits, motivation to serve, especially in risky combat positions, will diminish. While this republican model of committing oneself to the state in the form of military service still has strong societal support, cracks in the loyalty of the citizens towards the state in relation to this are becoming more and more visible. The Ashkenazi secular middle class in particular,[1] who used to form the core of the military, is drawing away as the benefits it can get through serving dwindle. Other peripheral groups, however, such as new immigrants and Oriental Jews are taking its place (see Levy 2003, 2006). These groups can still obtain social mobility through their service in the combat unit previously manned by the Ashkenazi elite and through their service hope to 'portray themselves as the new, true patriots' (Levy and Mizrahi 2008: 38).

The cracks in the loyalty towards the military become especially visible when one looks at the phenomenon of 'grey refusal', which Levy and Mizrahi characterized as one of a few possible 'quasi-exit strategies of alternative politics' (2008). They define grey refusal as an implicit refusal, usually achieved through informal arrangements with commanders when

---

1. Ashkenazi Jews are mostly Jews from European countries, or descendants of them, as opposed to the Sephardic or 'Oriental' Jews coming from the 'East'; meaning the Middle East and North Africa.

it comes to sensitive operations soldiers prefer not to engage in. However, the term is often used in a broader sense to include all instances of refusal to serve that are not explicitly conscientious, such as medical exemptions that are really politically or economically motivated (e.g. Sandler 2003). While explicit conscientious objection is quite rare and demands a high personal price, grey refusal is more widespread in Israel (Linn 1996). It is, however, not quantifiable as we cannot say with certainty what 'real' motivations lie behind not serving. Nevertheless, the fact that more and more young people opt out of service in order to pursue other avenues in life is an indicator of the dwindling loyalty, although still modest, to the military.

Despite these cracks, the military is still extremely important for Israeli society. As Helman writes, the 'sustained participation of Israeli-Jewish males in the military rests upon its construction in terms of a community ... belonging to this community of warriors is experienced in terms of embeddedness in society, as a criterion of normalcy and as an entitlement that legitimizes participation in the associations of civil society' (Helman 1997: 306). With this she emphasizes the dominance men have within the Israeli military and the way the Israeli state is able to create an image of the IDF as a natural phase in a young man's life.

Some elements of militarism in Israel are obvious and are easy to see or notice. There are, however, many characteristics of the Israeli militarized society that are political and thus not visible at first sight. Military service and rank during one's conscription, especially as professional military personnel, has a great influence on occupational possibilities in civilian life. Men benefit from this fact almost exclusively: '[O]ne of the results of this marginality of Jewish-Israeli women in the most important Israeli cultural and power institution – the military – is not only the reinforcement of women's marginality in society but also their exclusion from the most important societal discourse, that of "national security"' (Kimmerling 1993: 216–17). Thus women are excluded from important positions within the military and they take this marginality into civil society where work possibilities are linked to one's military career (see also Izraeli 2004 and Herzog 1998).

From an early age, Israeli children are familiarized with things military and with concepts such as security and war. The educational system in Israel is full of references to the military. It is not uncommon, for example, to see young children, four or five years old, going on school trips to military museums where warplanes and tanks are on display. Furthermore, soldiers, usually women, come to schools to teach as part of their national service. On national holidays, children make drawings and packages at school to send to the soldiers out at the front in order to demonstrate their support. The presence of the military and the concept of being a soldier are, then, normalized cognitively from a very early age.

This process of the 'normalization' of the presence of military often takes place in the form of rituals and ceremonies, for example during the celebration of national, Jewish holidays in which collective memories are constructed (see Furman 1999; Ben-Amos and Bet-El 1999). The educational framework in Israel, in Furman's eyes, 'display[s] two parallel, even contradictory trends: a collectivist orientation that prepares the child for future military roles, and an individualistic thrust that seeks to prepare the child for civilian life' (Furman 1999: 142). This first trend is very important. It points to a conscious effort by the Israeli state to construct myths and stories of collective identification within its educational system in order to ensure the continuing existence of loyal citizens who are willing to serve the state. In these myths and stories, furthermore, the Israeli self is portrayed as a victim who needs to protect him/herself and never as an aggressor.

Ideas about the Palestinian 'Other'

An important issue in the context of contemporary Israel as a militarized society concerns the processes of 'othering' vis-a-vis the Palestinian or Arab 'other'. In Israel there is a 'significant other' (Triandafyllidou 1998) unifying all different Jewish groups in society (such as Mizrahi Jews, Ashkenazi Jews, immigrants from Ethiopia and the Soviet Union). Opposed to the idealized, solidified, militarized collective of Jewish Israel stands this other; unmistakably 'the Palestinian' or, more commonly, 'the Arab'. In the construction of a national Jewish identity in Israel, which needed to be solidified and strong, the construction of a clearly defined 'other' was necessary because no boundary consolidation is really possible without someone standing outside of these boundaries.

Bar-Tal calls this a process of de-legitimization; 'the majority of Israeli Jews believe the ultimate objective of Palestinians is the annihilation of Israel and the establishment of a Palestinian state' (Bar-Tal 1990: 70) thus de-legitimizing them as 'others'. Marton has furthermore emphasized the prevalence of processes of 'splitting' within Israeli society, which reduce the Israeli worldview to something 'sharply divided into us Israelis – right and just – and them Palestinian – wrong and evil' (Marton 2008: 3). Through such processes the Israeli self is, furthermore, seen as an ultimate victim (ibid.).

This otherness of 'the Arab' or Palestinian is enforced through the strong emphasis Israeli society puts on Western culture as the 'proper' Israeli culture, largely dismissing Oriental or Arab Jewish culture as well as Palestinian culture as 'matter out of place' (Douglas 2002; see also Shohat 1999). Education within Israel does not deal with Palestinian culture in depth and if it does 'the defining characteristic is stereotypical and ... negative images ... are attributed to them [Palestinians]' (Lomksy-Feder and Ben-Ari 2007: 7).

Furthermore, Israel is a segregated society; Jews and Palestinians (Israeli citizens) rarely live in the same city let alone in the same neighbourhood. Most Palestinians with Israeli citizenship live either in the 'triangle' in Northern Israel or in one of the Palestinian communities spread across the country. Only a few 'mixed' cities exist in Israel, and these are usually internally segregated, dividing Palestinian and Jewish communities.

In addition, a negative prejudice exists against the Muslim world as a whole within Israel. A clear emphasis is put on its development into a Western, modern state and on it being 'the only democracy in the Middle East'. As such, a very clear distinction is drawn between Israeli society and the Arab Muslim world around it, a distinction that Israeli soldiers take with them into the OPT. A survey from 1980 'indicated a stereotypical tendency among Israeli youngsters to view all Arabs, anywhere within the state of Israel and beyond, as a menacing and ill-intentioned collective' (Rabinowitz 2001: 65). Bar-Tal also indicates that 'the Israeli Jews, from the beginning of their encounters with Palestinians, viewed them as primitive, bandits, cruel mobs, and failed to recognize their national identity' (Bar-Tal 1990: 71). Although the survey Rabinowitz mentions, which triggered the appearance of the coexistence field in Israel (projects promoting coexistence between Israeli Jews and Palestinian citizens of Israel), took place some thirty years ago and despite the fact that Bar-Tal's work is fairly old as well, I believe this outcome is still, at least in part, valid for views about Palestinians today, especially during the years of both Intifadas (see also Lomsky-Feder and Ben-Ari 2007: 7).

Uprisings

Since the Six Day War in 1967 Israel occupies the West Bank and the Gaza strip, which it conquered from Jordan and Egypt respectively, and it also came to control its inhabitants, the Palestinians.[2] Most of these Palestinians were displaced after the independence war of 1948, in 1967 or in subsequent years. Today, some four million Palestinians live divided between these two territories (2.5 million in the West Bank, 1.5 million in the Gaza Strip). This occupation of the Territories by Israel resulted, as will be discussed shortly, in two massive uprisings by the Palestinians, the first in 1987 and the second in 2000. While the first two decades were relatively quiet, since the late 1980s it became increasingly harder for Israel to suppress nationalist feelings by the Palestinians and to keep its repressive measures unseen. Gordon has eloquently described the different modes of control Israel has used during the occupation, in which he makes a distinction between disciplinary power and bio-power, which Israel mostly used until the outbreak of the First Intifada, and

---

2. The term 'Palestinian' used to identify a certain people and to describe a feeling of sharing a common past and future has only been used widely since 1967 when the national identity of the Palestinians became more and more of an issue.

sovereign power, which Israel started to put on the foreground with the outbreak of the Second Intifada. A great difference between these modes of power and the way Palestinians were treated by the occupier, according to Gordon, is that in the early years of the occupation Israel was very interested in influencing the lives of the Palestinians and their ways of thought and thus normalizing the occupation. By the time of the Second Intifada, Israel was only interested in controlling Palestinian space and was not interested in Palestinian lives anymore (Gordon 2008).

In 1987 the First Intifada broke out and lasted until 1993. The word *Intifada* literally means 'uprising' in Arabic and this Palestinian struggle did indeed begin as a fairly spontaneous uprising against the Israeli occupation, which had existed for twenty years at that time (van Creveld 1998). In the years after the 1967 occupation, and especially during the late 1970s, more and more Jewish settlements were built in the OPT and roadblocks were increasingly erected, making movement through the Territories difficult. In fact almost all facets of Palestinian life were (and still are) controlled by the mechanisms of the Israeli state, which Gordon (2008) describes as an infrastructure of control.

The demonstrations of 1987 were sparked by a traffic accident in the Gaza Strip in which four Palestinians were killed. Unlike previous demonstrations, however, these did not die down, instead growing more and more severe in the days that followed (van Creveld 1998). In the beginning this Intifada was very decentralized and actions happened spontaneously on every street, together with more general civil disobedience in the form of boycotts and underground activities. Only in 1989 did the PLO manage to centralize the activities of the uprising (Andoni 2001). The Israeli Defence Forces did not know how to deal with these civilian outbursts of violence, especially during the early days. Rules about the behaviour of soldiers towards the Palestinian rioters were made and changed over and over again leaving the soldiers with a deep sense of uncertainty. One famous 'order' was from Yitzhak Rabin who mentioned during an interview that soldiers should break the bones of the demonstrators. From the beginning of that uprising up until today, however, the IDF has gained much experience in dealing with civilian populations amongst whom rioters and instigators of unrest can hide.

The Al-Aqsa Intifada

In the year 2000 after a provocative visit on 28 September to the Temple Mount in Jerusalem by Ariel Sharon, then the opposition leader heading the Likud party, the second uprising in the Palestinian Territories broke out. This visit was, however, just the spark for an uprising that had been in the offing for a long time and one 'should look beyond the sparks to the deeper factors that determined the sudden transition from a seemingly routinized system of control to widespread violence involving young men and women ready to give their lives for the sake of ending the status quo' (Hammami and Tamari 2001: 5).

The Second Intifada or as the Palestinians termed it the 'Al-Aqsa Intifada' was, then, seen as a strong sign marking the feelings of frustration and anger within the Palestinian society of the OPT combined with a feeling of disillusionment about the Oslo agreement of 1993, which did not bring about the changes it had promised (Pressman 2003). The policies of the Israeli military and state continued during the Oslo years (between 1993 and 2000) – more Jewish settlements in the OPT were built, Palestinian houses were demolished and land was expropriated. Furthermore, all the major borders were controlled by Israel, including the borders to Jordan and Egypt as well as to East Jerusalem and the internal borders within the Territories (ibid.).

The First and Second Intifada differed significantly in the way the conflict took shape. While the First Intifada consisted mostly of non-violent actions and civil disobedience with the occasional hurling of rocks and Molotov cocktails, during the 'Al-Aqsa Intifada' the Palestinians used more violent means, such as IEDs (Improved Explosive Device) and suicide bombs, on both military and civilian targets. Some commentators have blamed Israel for 'fanning the flames' of the conflict in the hope this would lead to a swift military victory (Gordon 2008: 198).

Also from the point of view of the IDF a big difference was noticeable in the way the uprising was perceived. In the first three months alone more than a million bullets were fired by Israeli troops. The uprising was identified in terms of a war and the IDF used material and manpower appropriate for such a conflict. Especially in the beginning, the Israeli strategy made use of a lot of force to come down hard on the protests and it resorted to the extensive use of snipers. Open fire regulations were unclear and changed from day to day, and as Gordon shows, the law was not seen as a restriction anymore for the violent measures the military took, such as the extrajudicial executions that started to take place (Gordon 2008).

In the following years, the situation on the ground became increasingly hard for the local population. Palestinian daily life is to this day controlled by Israel on almost every level; for example, simply travelling from one point to another means getting permits and going through checkpoints. Leaving the OPT is impossible for most Palestinians.

There is no agreement about when the Al-Aqsa Intifada ended and about whether the violence of the last few years should be considered part of it or part of a Third Intifada. Most, however, locate its end between 2004 and 2005. Nevertheless after more than ten years the cycle of violence seems self-reinforcing and (unfortunately) seems never to come to an end. It is, nonetheless, the bleak background to this study; a clearer picture of the reality of Israeli soldiers within this situation will be given throughout this work.

The Al Aqsa Intifda as Asymmetrical Conflict

When investigating the behaviour and experiences of Israeli soldiers serving within this Intifada, it is important to look at the sort of conflict it is and how it is perceived by Israel. The characteristics of such a conflict heavily influence the way soldiers use violence and how they perceive the 'other' side; the Palestinians. Gordon has shown, and as was mentioned earlier, that the Al-Aqsa Intifada signified a change in Israeli strategies. Israel was no longer interested in controlling the lives of Palestinians, but only their movement; it wanted to control Palestinian space (Gordon 2008). While Israeli soldiers serve at the boundaries of this space when they man checkpoints and patrol roads and thus do directly control Palestinian lives, the overall idea of Israel was that of separation. If one did not leave their village, one did not have to meet the Israeli occupier (ibid.).

How can this Intifada then be characterized in terms of types of conflict used by military historians and strategists? In the years before the Cold War, nation-states in the West were engaged in so-called 'all-out wars'. This concept refers to 'classical' wars between the militaries of different nation-states, usually concerning border and ideological issues. 'The conflict that is characteristic of classical wars has a core of activity that takes the form of a series of clashes between professional organizations of combatants. These clashes take place in battle fields away from areas of non-combatant work and residence' (Kasher and Yadlin 2005: 7). This concept of war is easily grasped by outsiders but also by the soldiers involved. There are clear lines between sides within the conflict and clear goals to aim at.

However, with the end of the Cold War in 1989, massive battles between Western military forces are no longer to be expected. The conflicts that arise today are much more complex, involving numerous sides that often do not have regular, uniformed and recognizable militaries. Militants who are not distinguishable from civilians take part in such conflicts. Furthermore, soldiers are now regularly engaged in constabulary tasks, performing duties that were not part of soldiering in the Cold War era. The nature of conflict changed and became more ambiguous after 1989. It is no longer clear who exactly is the enemy and where he or she is situated and what kind of action is expected of the soldiers of regular armies, for example, when they face a civilian population with militants in its midst. Such conflicts are referred to as 'New Wars' (Kaldor 2006) or, for example, 'Fourth Generation Warfare', a term coined by Lind, Nightengale, Schmitt, Sutton and Wilson (1989) to denote a kind of warfare where national boundaries are dissolved into cultural or religious entities.[3] Where the 'distinction between war and peace

---

3. The Vietnam War, which also involved confrontations with civilians in a guerrilla war, is generally not seen as a case of 'Fourth Generation Warfare' because of the massive battles that took place between two conventional armies. Also, the US Army did not have any constabulary tasks in Vietnam.

[is] blurred to the vanishing point ... the distinction between "civilian" and "military" may disappear' (Lind et al. 1989: 23). Shamir and Ben-Ari further emphasize the 'blurring of the conventional concepts of "front" and "front-line battles" and ... the distinction between civilian and military' (1999: 15). They especially focus on the new kinds of military leadership that are necessary within such a changing field of conflict.

The term that I will use to typify the Al-Aqsa Intifada is 'asymmetrical conflict'. This type of conflict brings moral ambiguity and complexity with it. Importantly, the asymmetry in the conflict between Israel and the Palestinians is, first of all, one of means of organization. The Israeli side has a military with a vast array of weaponry, fighter jets, tanks and money from the Israeli state to back up its operations, not to mention the support of a relatively stable government and foreign financial aid. On the Palestinian side, the Palestinian fighters are relatively unorganized; at most they belong to one of the militias (which also often fight each other) or to one of the political parties that exist within the OPT. Their access to weaponry and financial means is limited and the political structure within their society is very unstable. The Palestinian Authority has been made powerless and even, some argue, an extension of Israeli security apparatus (Gazit 2009; Dekker 2011).

On a different level there exists an 'inherent imbalance in power between Israeli soldiers and Palestinian civilians' (Maoz 2001: 244). By looking at daily life in the OPT, it becomes obvious that there is a great power asymmetry: Israel is a powerful occupying force and the Palestinian citizens are virtually powerless. As mentioned before, Palestinians are at the mercy of the Israeli military on many different levels of their everyday lives.

A third characteristic of the conflict making it asymmetrical is the nature of the operations of the Israeli military as an occupation force. These operations tend to push soldiers into constabulary roles that involve intense contact with a civilian population. The Israeli military man checkpoints, patrol the streets and conduct house and body searches, activities for which soldiers usually are not specifically trained. Examples are soldiers who are instructed to maintain the closure of a village or town while being confronted with ambulances that urgently need to get through a checkpoint. In these confusing and complex situations, decisions have to be made on the spot, introducing an element of moral complexity to soldiers' tasks that are absent in 'classic' warfare.

Looking at the specific case of the 'Al-Aqsa Intifada' discussed above, it is, thus, a very clear case of an asymmetrical conflict, which is 'difficult to define ... as a "war" because there are no clear state boundaries and because there is almost no use of conventional fighting techniques such as artillery and long, swift, armoured manoeuvres' (Ben-Shalom, Lehrer and Ben-Ari 2005: 66). Furthermore, 'both sides are very different from each other in terms of their military power and potential and of their aims and modes of operation' (ibid.). Here it has, for instance, to be noted that on the side of the Palestinians the boundary between combatants/militants and civilians/non-combatants becomes very blurred, adding to the insecurity of the other side. Besides the constabulary tasks Israeli soldiers are sent to perform, however, they also find themselves in battles that can be rather intense (ibid.), battles such as Operation Defensive Shield in 2002, which will be discussed later on.

Soldiers as Perpetrators

In this work I theorize about Israeli soldiers, whose behaviour I'm trying to fathom, as perpetrators. This choice asks for some explanation. While in many instances of conflict it is not necessarily clear who is the victim and who is the perpetrator, especially in cases of asymmetrical conflict such as the Intifada (Maoz 2001: 246), in this study I will frame the group that, in the situation of the social encounter, performs acts of violence or harassment and that is in control over another group as perpetrator. Furthermore, I will deal with strategies of legitimization and disengagement employed by soldiers, and in the literature on these subjects an analytical opposition is made between perpetrator and victim. Thus, Israeli soldiers whose often violent behaviour is the focus of this research are framed as perpetrators in an analytical sense. The term 'perpetrator' is, then, used in a decriminalized manner. This does not, however, simply imply that none of the actions of the soldiers are criminal or illegal, just that they are not necessarily so. The soldiers are, nonetheless, the executors of violence or harassment vis-a-vis Palestinian civilians.

Misbehaviour and Violence

In recent years humiliating conduct or misconduct by Israeli security forces (i.e. soldiers and military policemen) has starkly increased, according to many human rights organizations who monitor such incidents, and who have observed that this behaviour has become part of the norm within the conduct of soldiers and hence is often not exposed (see, for example, reports by B'tselem, Human Rights Watch, Physicians for Human Rights-Israel and MachsomWatch). The behaviour described in those reports stands in stark contrast to the image the Israeli state and military want to promote to the outside world. The Israeli Defence Forces (IDF) is portrayed as 'one of the most moral militaries in the world' and certainly the most moral one in the Middle East. As more and more stories about misbehaviour of soldiers are reported by the press, human rights organizations and soldiers themselves,[4] the state and the military find themselves in need to react. This reaction usually

---

4. See the organization Breaking the Silence, www.breakingthesilence.org.il as accessed on 2 October 2012.

consists of strategies to explain and legitimize soldiers' conduct. Usually strategies emphasizing the exceptional nature of misbehaviour ('it was an isolated incident') or of contextualization and uniqueness ('the country finds itself in a very specific situation') are used to justify such behaviour, as already mentioned before (Cohen 2001: 109–10).

In this work I am specifically concerned with the daily behaviour of soldiers, which in their own eyes can be seen as normal but which is often contested by Human Rights organizations and basically unacceptable and/or disrespectful even if legal by law or according to military policies. These activities frequently concern a civilian population and are not so much encounters with a clear enemy, a characteristic of 'asymmetrical conflict' discussed above. The greatest friction between Israeli soldiers and Palestinians does not occur during military combat operations, but between soldiers and civilians at places like the checkpoints of the West Bank.

It is important at this stage to clarify exactly what I mean when speaking of misbehaviour, as it can take many forms. Within this work I will use this term when speaking about recognized illegal acts or physical violence (according to army regulations and the code of conduct), and to indicate acts of humiliation, daily harassment and verbal aggression, all of which occur on a daily basis in the OPT. These acts and use of violence are often not seen as real misbehaviour by soldiers and their commanders, as they occur daily and often do not result in anyone getting physically hurt. Indeed, such acts almost never, even if in clear violation of the law, make it to court and soldiers and officers responsible are rarely punished (see also Gordon 2008 on the withdrawal of the law from the OPT during the Al-Aqsa Intifada). Often such acts are not even in conflict with military orders and are seen as completely legitimate.

Soldiers' conduct is often inherently violent. But it is important here to look for a moment at the distinction between 'legal' or 'legitimate' violence by soldiers, such as referred to above, and illegal violence and misbehaviour by soldiers. The first falls within the scope of orders that are given to soldiers and the second concerns their over-aggressiveness during the performance of their tasks. One could say that the latter kind of behaviour is, in comparison to the first, of an immoral nature. The Israeli military is strongly aware of issues of military ethics and the official orders and subsequent behaviour of soldiers should, in theory, be in line of at least these ethical guidelines.[5]

---

5. The IDF has an ethical code, named 'The Spirit of the IDF' written by philosopher Asa Kasher, which regulates soldiers' behaviour in terms of their behaviour within the military (comradeship, responsibility, discipline, etc.) but also emphasizes the importance of human life and the 'purity of arms' principle, which tells soldiers to only use their weapons in self-defence, see also http://dover.idf.il/IDF/English/about/doctrine/ethics.htm as accessed on 29 May 2012.

However, while we would like to believe that soldiers will at all times act morally and we try to train them as such, within the context of asymmetrical conflict ethical behaviour is a complex issue. As I argue in this study, the behaviour of soldiers depends on many more factors than on the moral rules they have learned during basic training. Decisions often have to be made in the spur of a moment and circumstances are confusing at best.

Furthermore, orders by IDF officers that are given to soldiers often vary largely across the board. Orders are given ad-hoc by officers and NCOs and frequently very low-level commanders have a great say in how activities are performed on a ground level, for example at the checkpoint. Thus it can well be that a checkpoint commander orders the soldiers to stop all men trying to go through and detain them for a few hours without a clear explanation. This is an order given by a superior to his soldiers, however, does this mean it is a moral act? And not only on this low level is the morality of military orders unclear, on high levels, at times, orders are given for activities and the use of weapons that are characterized by international law as crimes of war. However, Israel often claims such activities or weapons are needed in self-defence or denies them altogether.[6]

Thus the definition of an order of a superior as moral is questionable, first of all because the borders of morality are contextual and vague, especially within conflict. Second, we have to accept the fact that orders are always given by people (orders that themselves can also be immoral of course), and people are prone to behave against rules that have been set out. Soldiers can then receive 'immoral' (meaning against the 'Spirit of the IDF') orders by their superiors and they will obey them as they have learned to do. While the IDF knows the concept of the illegal order that soldiers may not obey, in practice not one soldier has ever been protected by this rule and most have been punished for disregarding an order. In Minow's words, soldiers at time get the confusing message that tells them 'you should resist an illegal order unless you cannot – however, people later will assess whether you could not' (Minow 2007: 26). Another example within the Israeli case is the order many IDF soldiers received to 'confirm kills'. This concept that relates to making sure an enemy shot is really dead is illegal, but many soldiers have testified they were specifically told and taught to do so.[7]

---

6. See for example the reports on the use of white phosphor by Israeli troops in Gaza in 2008–09. The use was at first denied by Israel, but clearly proven by parties such as Human Rights Watch, www.hrw.org/news/2009/03/25/israel-white-phosphorus-use-evidence-war-crimes as accessed on 11 May 2012. When faced with the evidence Israel said it would start an investigation into the improper use of this chemical.
7. See for example testimonies collected by Breaking the Silence, www.breakingthesilence.org.il/testimonies/database/?ci=126 as accessed on 12 May 2012.

There are of course also soldiers who go beyond the orders they receive and are overly aggressive out of their own free will. These soldiers 'vent' their frustrations, their racist ideas perhaps or copy the behaviour of others. But their behaviour can also be a result of the kind of work they perform and, as I will argue in this work, their subsequent blurred moral vision.

In this work a lot will be said on these issues and the circumstances that influence the behaviour of soldiers during their service. Here it is important to emphasize that when I speak about misbehaviour of soldiers, I will both speak of behaviour that is the result of 'legal' orders and activities that are violent beyond military orders. The boundaries between both kinds of behaviour, for the sake of the argument of this work, are too blurred and unclear to be of meaning. My interest lays in uncovering the multitude of factors influencing the behaviour of soldiers on the basis of their own accounts. Thus the focus will be on the meaning these young men give to their experiences and behaviour, and on their own definition of what is 'legal' or 'illegal' behaviour, 'moral' or 'immoral' conduct.

Conclusion

Instead of looking at the situational effects on the work of soldiers from a macro point of view as many works have done, this study will take an anthropological bottom-up stance and will distil from observations and interviews with soldiers the way they give meaning to their surroundings. Focusing on spatial effects of the work environment on the soldiers adds a new dimension to existing work that tries to understand their (mis) behaviour.

This work will show how these spatial surroundings of Israeli soldiers, called work arenas in this study, provide the circumstances for processes of numbing on different levels, resulting in moral numbing and an increased chance to the use of violence and other kinds of misbehaviour. By closely examining the circumstances under which soldiers work, the way they talk about it and the meanings they give to their own behaviour, this study will offer new insights on how we can understand soldiers within modern-day conflict.

CHAPTER 2

STUDYING SOLDIERS

In this chapter I will frame my argument theoretically. First of all, I perceive this work as being part of a small but growing field of the anthropology of morality. Many anthropologists have concerned themselves with what is perceived as 'good' or 'bad' in different cultures and what people, according to their beliefs, ought to or ought not to do. Without describing their work in such terms, the study of these anthropologists dealt with issues of morality. Mead already 'suggested that every human group has separate sets of behaviour for the treatment of in-group members and out-group members', clearly referring to group morality (in Cohen et al. 2006: 1560).

However, as Zigon rightly argues, we should be careful with contributing the term 'anthropology of morality' to any work concerning itself with religion, kinship or other 'socially approved habits' as Benedict called them (Zigon 2008). Zigon warns us, furthermore, not to confuse things we as anthropologists call 'morality' with things our interlocutors would label as such. In this work the focus is indeed on morality as the researcher perceives it analytically and not necessarily as the informants would phrase it. I will use a broad definition of morality that includes most thoughts, deliberations and activities of soldiers that, as they involve an 'other', can be defined as inherently moral. How soldiers behave towards this other, the Palestinian in this case, how they explain their behaviour and relate about it are all included when speaking about soldiers' morality. As Edel and Edel stated 'a great part of any morality must be articulated in discourse' (1959: 108) and they thus urge us to look at 'patterns of argumentation, teaching and justification' when we study morality (ibid.). Something I will also do in this study.

The amount of anthropological work on moralities is not extensive and the current project will be able to contribute to this niche while using the above-mentioned approach, focusing on the moralities of Israeli soldiers during their tour of duty in the Occupied Palestinian Territories. It is *not* an effort to produce an ethnography of Israeli morality, its primary aim being to outline moralities within the Israeli military context, to see how they are shaped by space soldiers control and how these moralities are articulated in the words of soldiers, and through this to learn about their ideas and behaviour while serving in the Territories.

Becoming or Being a Perpetrator

In order to successfully make my argument it is important to frame it within existing work on perpetrators and their use of violence. On the most basic level it is imperative to state here that my argument is in line with the many scholars who believe that the violent behaviour of perpetrators, sometimes even falling within the category of atrocities, is a consequence of circumstantial factors and not (solely) of individual characteristics on the side of the perpetrator. Zimbardo (2007) makes a distinction in this line between dispositional factors and situational factors. The first one is the belief that deeds are only to be accredited to the individual who should have complete responsibility over his or her actions. This is in fact exactly the way military and political leaders in Israel react to the misbehaviour of soldiers; the already discussed 'rotten apple' metaphor. Only the individual is judged, the (social) circumstances are not scrutinized. Taking his famous Stanford prison experiment as a starting point, Zimbardo argues for a situational approach, where one does not stare blindly upon inner determinants of personal behaviour but mostly on the outer ones. These 'outer determinants' he categorizes as 'place' and 'situation' under which we can find roles people take on, norms, anonymity of persons and places, dehumanizing processes, pressures, group identity and many more (Zimbardo 2007: 197).

Zimbardo is not alone is this position. Many works that have been written about perpetrators of violence, especially in relation to the Second World War, have similar arguments. A well-known example is the work of Browning (1992) who analyzes the stories of policemen of the Reserve Police Battalion 101 serving in Poland who killed numerous innocent Jews in short bloody military actions. The title of his book makes his position clear, *Ordinary Men*, with which he points out the uncomfortable truth that most horrific deeds by men are not done by sadists or monsters, but by 'normal' human beings who were able to commit such acts because of the (many) specific circumstances they found themselves in.

While the work of Browning was discredited by Goldhagen (1996) a few years after it came out with a cultural argument and the premise that what happened in the Second World War was unique in its specific time and space, most scholars who worked on these major questions have agreed on the 'situational theory' (see, for example, Smeulers 2004; Staub 1989; Smeulers and Grünfeld 2011), which I will also take as the starting point for my work. I will thus not perceive the situation in the OPT and the behaviour of Israeli soldiers within it as a unique case, but rather as a case that can shed light on other, comparable cases elsewhere because of the major role of situational factors on soldiers' behaviour.

Soldiers' Misconduct and Use of Violence

The behaviour of soldiers has been of interest to many scholars in the past and to this day. Much has been written about Hitler's soldiers in the Second World War and of course also the Vietnam War has been the subject of many works that were keen to understand how soldiers could carry out the often horrendous acts they committed. Recently, the behaviour of US soldiers in Iraq and Afghanistan has been a topic of great interest in this field. These works, of which a few will be discussed here, can give us important insights about the different circumstances and characteristics of conflict and war that influence the (moral) behaviour of soldiers. I will here set apart the most important circumstances that are attributed in the literature to influencing soldiers' conduct and their use of violence, in order to give some specific background to this work and, most importantly, to show the theoretical position of this work within this body of literature.

The first 'case', one that can be even seen as the starting point of works on perpetrators' behaviour, is the Second World War. As already mentioned above, works on this war and the horrendous acts of Nazi soldiers and commanders have predominantly concluded that the behaviour of these perpetrators was not a matter of being some kind of monster, but the workings of 'normal' German citizens (Arendt 1963; Browning 1992; Staub 1989). Arendt (1963) was the first one who shocked the world with her idea on the 'banality of evil' and thus the fact that one does not have to be a monster in order to do evil. She emphasized the absence of critical thinking and the uncritical following of orders as one of the main reasons for the holocaust, not a specific kind of 'evil' that the Nazis possessed. In his analysis of *The Roots of Evil* (1989), Staub speaks of a 'continuum of destruction' in order to show how genocide and mass killings can become acceptable by taking 'little steps' along a continuum of acceptance. Killing one time makes the next time easier, accepting certain benefits from the system (such as the Nazi party) changes something in a person, which makes the next step, for example firing Jews from a workplace, easier. Staub encourages us to look at circumstances and the personality of a person (in Staub's definition also ideology for example), the system they are part of and forces that play a role in perpetrators' behaviour (1989: 144). In Nazi Germany a combination of feelings of superiority of the Germans and feelings of threat and insecurity, anti-Semitism, a strong culture of obedience to authority, a monolithic-totalitarian culture and a strong ideology 'helped' the perpetrators to commit their crimes (ibid.: 233).

In his famous work on Battalion 101, Browning cites the wide racist and anti-Semitic propaganda Nazi perpetrators were immersed in as very influential. He, furthermore, emphasizes the training of the police unit he studied, but he especially looks at the conformity to the group, not wanting to break the ranks, which he believes had a very important influence on the ability of the members of the unit to kill Jews in massive killing sprees. The policemen, should they refuse, would be completely isolated and would lose their social world (Browning 1992: 184–05).

The main issues that are thus highlighted by the studies of Staub and Browning are the importance of social background, ideology and the military socialization of Nazi soldiers in explaining their willingness to kill in such numbers and in such ways as they did. Works on the Vietnam War and most importantly the My Lai massacre by US soldiers add another dimension to the analysis. *Crimes of Obedience* is one of the most famous works on this issue. Taking the My Lai massacre as a case in point, Kelman and Hamilton (1989) study the way obedience in war can lead to gross human rights violations. They describe how crimes of obedience become possible when 'individuals [soldiers] abandon personal responsibility for actions taken under superior orders continuing to obey when they ought to be disobeying' (1989: 20). What happens is that when someone gets an order from a trusted authority, this order is taken as moral and just and thus personal responsibility is forsaken.

Recently this body of works is enriched with work by scholars who have extensively discussed the behaviour of US soldiers in Iraq and Afghanistan, especially after the Abu Ghraib incident that was publicized in 2004. In court the behaviour of the soldiers who tortured Iraqi prisoners and forced them to perform humiliating tasks while photographing them, was viewed as 'the sadistic work of a few rogue soldiers' (Zimbardo 2007: xiii). As already shown before, many scholars investigating perpetrators' behaviour do not agree with such a simplistic explanation for committing atrocities. The court case triggered Zimbardo to, finally, write his book on the Stanford prison experiment in order to prove this discourse faulty and to emphasize the power of the system a soldier is in on his or her behaviour. In his analysis of the Abu Ghraib prison, he looks at the space, the history and the politics behind this institution, at the person involved (Chip Frederick, the staff sergeant who worked in the prison) and the activities the soldiers had to perform with all circumstantial characteristics present.

All three of these cases and their analysis thus can help us to understand how Israeli soldiers can act in the ways they are reported to do. Following the discussed studies their behaviour should be analyzed on a situational and systemic level; one should look at their ideological background, their relationships with their comrades and their superiors, group cohesion and obedience and at the dynamics of the military itself.

The Israeli Case

In order to get closer to the particulars of the Israeli case, I will now look more closely at scholarly work that indeed, as suggested above, looks at outside factors in order to understand Israeli soldiers and their behaviour. Gordon (2008) shows in his important work *Israel's Occupation* how the use of different forms of control Israel has been using during its occupation of the OPT has influenced the situation on the ground and the way force and power are used against the Palestinian people. From operating according to the 'colonization principle' within which the colonization of territory is normalized and made invisible as much as possible, the occupation today works according to a separation principle where the land and the people living on it are separated as entities of different interest of Israeli policy (Gordon: xix). This transfer from deeply controlling individual's lives to a sheer lack of interest in the Palestinian people while focusing on colonized resources has a great influence on the way the occupation is carried out and thus the conduct of soldiers as agents of this occupation.

Gordon distinguishes between three different modes of power in use by Israel in the OPT: disciplinary, bio and sovereign power. The first one is defined as imposing homogeneity on people from below in such ways as to make them docile. Bio-power is often used with disciplinary power and it deals with the population as a whole. Through controlling institutions involved in medical care, economy and welfare, for example, Israel controls the population and keeps track of birth/death rates, distribution of labour, income and other kinds of population data (ibid.: 12). These two modes of power, disciplinary and bio, have been used in the aftermath of the Six-Day War in 1967 when Israel had just occupied Gaza and the West Bank. The idea was to normalize the occupation: '[B]y boosting the economy and producing prosperity ... a great deal of energy was invested in reshaping the collective identity of the population and suppressing Palestinian nationalism' (ibid.: 13).

In more recent years, during the Al-Aqsa Intifada and afterwards, Israel started to focus on a more traditional way of controlling the occupied population through a mode of sovereign power. Gordon defines this mode as 'the imposition of a legal system and the employment of the state's police and military to either enforce the rule of law or to suspend it' (ibid.: 13). Palestinian resistance was with no exception interpreted as terrorism, Israel was no longer interested in keeping the occupation 'invisible' and an increasing amount of aggression was to be used by military troops to suppress terror. In order to do so a whole system of checkpoints was put into place, soldiers were sent on patrolling missions into villages, towns and between them and movement of Palestinian citizens was severely restricted by a system of permits that were to be issued by the Israeli military.

Importantly, this also meant that more lethal violence was used against the Palestinian population than before. Gordon shows that especially Operation Defensive Shield is an example of this change; more remote and lethal weaponry was used (aircraft, tanks), violence was also used against offices of the PA (Palestinian Authority), thus against the management of the population, and the Palestinian infrastructure was targeted (Gordon 2008: 204).

Gordon gives us insights into the system within which the soldiers serve who feature in this work. The policies he describes dictate the sort of activities soldiers are told to perform; indeed they shape the space where soldiers sit out their tours of duty.

The modes of power used by the state are closely connected to the character of the conflict itself. While modes of power are used by the occupying party, the form a conflict takes is not only a product hereof, but also of the way the occupied party reacts to this occupation. Earlier, I have characterized the Al-Aqsa Intifada as an asymmetrical conflict to emphasize the asymmetry between both parties, Israel and the Palestinians and to illuminate the unclear categories that are at the core of this conflict. Ron (2003) has categorized the situation in Gaza and the West Bank as 'ghettos' in contrast to frontier conflicts such as the war with Lebanon. He argues that depending on the sort of conflict a state is waging, it will use more or less violence against the people it fights against or whose territory it occupies. In relation to this categorization, Gordon (2008) has rightly argued that in the case of the West Bank the idea of the ghetto/ frontier division only applies up to the Al-Aqsa Intifada. Up until that time the occupying force, as mentioned above, was interested in controlling the lives of the Palestinians. However, as Gordon argues, since the outbreak of the last Intifada Israel is less interested in this kind of control and more in a sovereign kind. It does, however, and this point is central in the argumentation of Gordon, control Palestinian space very thoroughly (think of the enclavization of Palestinian land [see Falah 2005] and the wall that surrounds the West Bank). Thus using Ron's conceptualization, Gordon argues that during the last decade the Territories have become ghettos space wise, but frontiers when looking at institutional control of Israel over the Palestinian people. Again, this is a crucial insight if we want to understand the ways soldiers operate within an occupation and the ways they are militarily socialized to think about the 'other'.

These works are then valuable for their insights into the modes of power used by Israel and the kind of violence the state uses in specific kinds of conflict, relating to institutional control and space and the way an occupation is administered. This has direct consequences for the tasks soldiers are asked to perform and on the spaces they find themselves in during their conscription, such as checkpoints and patrols. In fact, where these works end, this work will continue; it will try to understand more thoroughly what it means to be a soldier carrying out the policies that are analyzed by Gordon and Ron to see exactly how the spaces, which are the outcome of the modes of power discussed, influence the (moral) behaviour of Israeli conscripts. Before doing this, I want to go one level down in abstraction and look at work that has focused on features of the Israeli military itself in relation to Israeli society, such as competitiveness, which are said to influence soldiers' use of violence or aggression.

In his elaborate work on the Israeli military Yagil Levy has, amongst other theories, coined the ideas of convertibility and competition over symbolic rewards. Convertibility is related to the relationship that exists in Israel between doing military service and the two different types of rewards one can get for it in civilian life; material rewards (payment, pension and the like) and symbolic rewards (such as prestige and honour) (Levy 2007: 189). Levy has showed how these symbolic rewards have differed for diverse (ethnic) groups in Israel, with the Ashkenazi elite getting a higher reward than Oriental immigrants, for example, who were marginalized and did not serve in prestigious combat units. However, this has changed over the years as the abovementioned elite demands more for their input in the military (as combatants), and many have opted out as they can get their rewards much easier in civilian life, such as through the educational system. For the Oriental and Russian migrants it is a different story and they filled in the gaps left vacant by the Ashkenazi elite as they still had a lot to gain (in civilian life) from military service (Levy 2008).

This change in social composition of combat units has influenced the aggression of soldiers, Levy argues, which brings me to his second point. While Levy also acknowledges the change in attitude of the state and military towards the Palestinians, he has also observed a change in the *motivation* of soldiers to fight. In the Al-Aqsa Intifada soldiers seemed over motivated, which caused more aggressive conduct (ibid.: 1584). Because of the fierce competition over symbolic rewards between social groups in the military, Levy argues, soldiers become over motivated to hang on to their positions. Soldiers become less critical of the ethical problems they are confronted with (in comparison to soldiers in the First Intifada). This competition 'intensifies the significance of battlefield achievements as the supreme test of fighting and might' (ibid.).

These scholars have given us several explanations for the use of violence by Israeli soldiers in recent years. By looking at the modes of power Israel uses, the kind of conflict it is involved in (and thus the kind of operations its soldiers need to perform) and dynamics within the military, a lot becomes clear about the behaviour of Israeli soldiers. What is missing, however, is a bottom-up investigation of the way spaces soldiers work within shape their behaviour as well. This work then will bring a contribution to this body of work and will give new insights into how we can understand soldiers' behaviour, their use of violence and, importantly, the way the soldiers interpret their own behaviour and give voice to it.

Space, Power, (mis)Behaviour and Morality

The existing literature then looks at soldiers' use of violence and their aggression from different perspectives. What has not been studied often, however, is the influence space has on the work of soldiers, their (mis) behaviour and the moralities they construct. In this work then, as stated before, I will emphasize this influence by closely looking at the spaces Israeli soldiers work within and the way these spaces shape their doings and discourse.

That space is not just a container of our actions has become clear from studies of philosophers like Foucault (1995) and Lefebvre (2007) and anthropologists like Augé (1995). In Lefebvre's words, we produce space as a social construct. His main argument is that there are three distinct moments in the production of space; representation of space (how planners for example vision it), representational space (for example by artists and photographers) where our imagination of space is central and, lastly, spatial practices, our actual lived experiences within space.

Space is thus about power, about who decides about the ways to use it (planning) and about the character it should ideally have. Lefebvre and also Augé both warn us of the impersonal characteristics of modern space, where the individual is forced into a specific mould by the ones in power. This relationship of space and power is crucial when connecting it to the use of violence, also a product of power. Working on this interface between space and the use of power, Herbert (1997) has written an insightful work on the way Los Angeles' police officers control space. He looked at their spatial strategies that according to him arise from different normative orders the officers work within. He makes use of Sack's (1986) definition of human territoriality as 'spatial strateg[ies] to affect, influence, or control resources and people by controlling area' (Herbert 1997: 3). While the context of Herbert's work is different than that of the Israeli military, his findings are very useful. He describes six normative orders that shape the practices of officers within space: law, bureaucratic regulation, adventure/machismo, safety, competence and morality. Israeli soldiers are subject to similar normative orders, albeit their meanings change according to the context. These soldiers are conscripts and not professional officers, they work within an occupation, not in their own territory and what forms one of the most important normative orders for them, as we shall see, are the commands they receive from their superiors. Hierarchy is crucial within their work. Nevertheless, the idea of normative orders shaping spatial strategies are useful in order to understand the activities of Israeli soldiers in depth.

Territoriality (Sacks 1986) is shaped by ideas policemen (or soldiers) have about the other, the orders they receive from above, their background and more of such 'normative orders' (Herbert 1997). Thus, as these works show us, not only is space (re)produced by us, space and the way it is formed also has a profound influence on our doings and on our (power) relationship with the other. If we translate these ideas to the focus of this work – we can say that the spaces soldiers move within are diverse – they will be framed and interpreted differently and thus will have different kinds of effects on their behaviour. Not only are they planned in specific ways (checkpoints for example), they are also imagined differently and consequently 'used' in different ways.

Physical Closeness and Distance

Another important factor when looking at space and its effect on soldiers' behaviour is proximity. The proximity of soldiers to 'the other', the Palestinians they meet on a daily basis at the checkpoints, in the cities or villages and in the Palestinian homes they enter. As we shall see, the degree of distance or proximity between both parties can have a profound effect on the moral behaviour of soldiers and on their (moral) decision making.

Two scholars on this issue, Vetlesen and Bauman, disagree on the way physical distance or proximity affects the behaviour of perpetrators towards their victims. Vetlesen (2005) believes that proximity between people does not make it more difficult to hurt a person. He distinguishes between physical proximity and the sense of feeling close to someone. Thus, when you know a person, it is harder to hurt him (or her) no matter what the physical distance between you is. Physical proximity/distance is, then, not enough to explain immoral behaviour or the avoidance of it; it is also important to look at the way we perceive this person and at our relationship with them. In Bauman's work (1989), Vetlesen argues, the notion of proximity is not explained and thus remains vague. Bauman does not take the psychic notion of proximity into account and draws a direct relation between spatial proximity and moral behaviour (in accordance with the famous experiments done by Milgram in 1974). Bauman, who like Vetlesen mostly focuses on the Holocaust, ignores, in Vetlesen's view, the ideological zest with which the Nazis worked to exterminate the Jews of Europe. Vetlesen concludes that 'proximity interacts with a number of factors; it does not by itself bring about, let alone account for, moral conduct or the lack of it' (2005: 27) thus adding an emotional charge to the notion of proximity.

In his influential work *On Killing*, Grossman writes extensively about the relationship between ways of killing an enemy and the emotional and physical distance from him or her. He contends that the greater the distance we find between ourselves and the enemy, the easier it is to kill him or her. However, he also discusses the issue of emotional distance in his work, and writes that 'there is a constant danger on the battlefield that, in periods of extended close combat, the combatants will get to know and acknowledge one another as individuals and subsequently may refuse to kill each other' (Grossman 1995: 158). Thus, getting to know and especially beginning to care about the other inevitably alters the way a soldier sees the enemy and the way he will treat him or her. In the case of Israeli soldiers this factor is maybe even stronger as they do not have combatants in front of them but mostly civilians. Seeing these people as 'individuals' with feelings can make it harder for the soldier to carry out work that essentially suppresses them.

I agree here with Vetlesen's ideas and with Grossman's work and hence try to keep the notion of 'othering' (Spivak 1985; Besteman 1996; Baumann and Gingrich 2006) in mind when looking at the effect of spatial distance between Israeli soldiers and Palestinian civilians. The concept of 'othering' can be used when analyzing the way different groups relate to each other negatively and especially the ways one group can 'other' another group in order to establish itself and distance itself from this 'other'. The way the soldiers feel towards the 'other' and the degree they feel closeness or distance to them should, then, be taken into account when looking at the issue of proximity and moral behaviour.

Constructed Moralities in Speech

The second part of the argument in this work concerns discursive, moral strategies or 'moralities' of soldiers. These moralities, I argue, are produced and shaped within the spaces soldiers move in with all the characteristics and effects that come with them. I want to show how Israeli soldiers use specific strategies to explain and legitimize their behaviour and experiences with violence. As already stated above, much has been written on questions of how people can commit violence or atrocities and how horrendous events such as genocides can take place (see, for example, Bauman 1989; Staub 1989; Vetlesen 2005). Such works, however, important as they are, often lack a specific focus on the spatial factors that can shape soldiers' behaviour and discourses, something this study will pick up. In this work I want to look at the way soldiers talk and explain about their behaviour and thus at the strategies they use when legitimizing their deeds.

Much of the psychological literature that focuses on explaining the reaction of people to traumatic events, such as witnessing grave suffering, often includes the works of S. and A. Freud, who both wrote about the defence mechanisms that come into play when people have to shield themselves off from something they have witnessed. These defence mechanisms were once accepted, within psychological theory, as being completely unconscious. People were believed to have internal mechanisms outside of their own control that served to block their consciousness for things that were too hard to grasp or too painful to see.

Today, more and more critical voices are heard, however, disputing the claim that these mechanisms are solely unconscious. In her work on the responses people give when confronted with human rights abuses and suffering, Seu warns us about this (2003). In her article she mentions psychological explanations that are used by lay people 'to justify indifference and lack of action' (2003: 184). Phrases such as 'shutting off, closing down, turning away, not wanting to know' (ibid.: 183) are used as defence mechanisms against the effects such suffering could have on the person witnessing it.

More importantly, in her work she argues for an understanding of a 'desensitized subject' or a person who views him or herself as getting an overload of information about suffering and who, accordingly, 'shuts off' or is desensitized as 'a psychological subject as well as morally agentic' (ibid.: 183). This means that explanations given by people who are confronted with the suffering of others about being desensitized, of 'shutting off' or of blocking the suffering out should not be taken at face value. Such explanations can easily be seen, Seu argues, as justifications for not taking action and for giving in to apathy. These people should be still seen as agents of their own actions and not as mere 'subjects' under the complete control of the effects of the suffering they have witnessed.

Cohen also argues that we should ask ourselves if shutting off is really as unconscious as it is made out to be. Denial, as he calls such mechanisms, is always partial. It is usually a case of not wanting to know anymore and of thus 'turning a blind eye' (Cohen 2001).

Seu and Cohen's realization that denial is partial and that a degree of consciousness is present when denying acts is important here. It seems too easy to use psychological theories of 'blocking out' or 'shielding off' to explain the acts of soldiers. Seeing them as moral agents within a specific context, who should be expected to be able to make moral decisions for themselves, is an important step in understanding soldiers' discourse and behaviour while not losing sight of the fact that this ability is heavily influenced by multiple other factors, such as the space they are part of and control, the type of conflict they fight within and the policies they are the 'product' of.

Moral Disengagement and Denial

To get back to psychological theory, the notion of moral reasoning has specifically been elaborated within this discipline. Kohlberg, a follower of Piaget, developed several theories and tests to capture moral judgements and moral motivations through scales and graphs (Kohlberg 1969, 1981, 1984).

Albert Bandura (1991) breaks away from this narrow position and includes social influences into his work to explain moral reasoning and also actual moral conduct. In his social cognitive theory he criticizes the way most stage theorists (such as Kohlberg) conduct their research with abstract moral situations that do not correspond to actual, real-life settings in which people are confronted with real moral issues.

The focus of Bandura is the capacity of people to refrain from amoral behaviour (moral agency) and the 'psychological manoeuvres by which moral self-sanctions are ... disengaged from inhumane conduct' (1999: 193) – moral disengagement. He places these issues within their social surroundings and thus claims to look at actual conduct instead of abstract situations.

Bandura's moral disengagement is a 'cognitive restructuring of inhumane conduct into a benign and or worthy one' (2002: 101) through several different mechanisms. Each of these mechanisms has as its goal to disengage oneself from self-sanctions, which we all have. Our self-sanctions, in general, keep our conduct in line with our internal standards, our values and morality. If we, through various mechanisms that will be discussed here, disengage from these self-sanctions, we are able to behave in ways that are different from what our internal values prescribe. This behaviour has a potential to be immoral and even violent.

As a psychologist, Bandura focuses on cognitive processes and he does not, therefore, give examples of the actual speech people use. His theory, however, involves strategies that feature in the accounts people give that can thus be seen as discursive strategies. He, however, does not analyze speech as such but rather theorizes about more general categories that can be used when analyzing this.

Missing in Bandura's work is, furthermore, the influence external spatial circumstances can have on people's conduct. Even though he breaks away from the work of Kohlberg (which does not take social circumstances into consideration) he could take this issue further himself. In this work, for example, we will see how feelings of boredom, frustration and attrition can have a profound influence on the way people, soldiers in this case, behave and make sense of their own behaviour and thus on the discursive and moral strategies they use.

The reason why his work is still important and helpful here is due to the fact that Bandura points out central themes that could help us recognize strategies in the speech of soldiers. He identifies several ways in which people disengage from their behaviour and these are very useful for further analysis.

Although Cohen (2001) is also concerned with strategies used when explaining immoral behaviour, he looks at this subject from a sociological point of view. More so than Bandura, he looks at the actual behaviour and speech of people and gives ample examples of these in his work. He, furthermore, dedicates space to the issue of bystanders; people who witness suffering and atrocities and their own actions or inaction. He thus connects his theory to real-life situations that are recognizable for most.

Cohen theorizes about the different states of denial human beings find themselves in or, better yet, create for themselves (2001). These states of denial can take place on a personal level but also on a political level and even on the level of a whole state or society. For our purposes, personal denial is the most interesting form as we are looking at soldiers' discourses.

However, as we shall see, soldiers at times adopt official or ideological language that is commonly used by institutions of the state.

What Cohen wants to find out is the way we are able to look away, be indifferent or stay silent in the face of suffering and atrocities. How can we know about such suffering and then claim not to know or, if we admit to knowing about it, not act upon this knowledge? In his work, Cohen identifies different methods of denial that people and states make use of, which can help us understand the language of justification, rationalization and normalization on a deeper level.

In Cohen's eyes 'statements of denial are assertions that something did not happen, does not exist, is not true or is not known about' (2001: 3). However, to act in denial could also be seen as 'the need to be innocent of a troubling recognition' (ibid.: 33). This means that we choose or want (in some way consciously) to stay in the dark about a fact or happening that is difficult to see or hear about and that could, were we to know about it, force us into some kind of action. His interpretation of denial is a broad one, from literal denial (denying any knowledge about something) to 'implicatory' denial (denial of the implications a certain act has, the act as such not being denied here).

Perpetrators' Accounts

Important is the realization that the speech acts of offenders can be interpreted and analyzed as accounts. Within these speech acts, the offender or bystander addresses accountability for the actions perpetrated or witnessed. This then becomes, Cohen asserts, a form of moral accounting (2001: 59).

These accounts are products of the social environment in which they are formed. This means that such accounts are not private and particular but part of a shared discourse. In different social settings, different accounts of the same events can be given, referring to the deep social character such accounts have.

As I am dealing with soldiers' explanations about their behaviour and their motivations for it, the realization that their accounts are social and influenced by their (spatial) surroundings is very important. Because accounts are 'embedded in popular culture, banal language codes and state-encouraged legitimations' (ibid.: 76), keeping the background of the Israeli soldiers in mind is imperative.

Cohen divides accounts into two categories: justifications and excuses. Users of the first category of accounts admit that an act was committed but refuse to see it as wrong. Such accounts are often ideological, aggressive and unapologetic (Cohen 2001: 59). Excuses try to neutralize and normalize the acts committed; they admit the wrongness of an act but add that they 'had to do it' or that they 'didn't have a choice' (ibid.). As we shall see, both categories will be found in the discourse of Israeli soldiers serving within the OPT.

The work of Bandura and Cohen, then, will be used in this work as a framework within which we can understand the way soldiers use moral strategies. This framework will then be used to make sense of the accounts of Israeli soldiers and the strategies they utilize.

Conclusion

In this chapter I have tried to frame my theoretical argument, which can be divided in two parts. However, I began by positioning this work within the debate on 'why and how' perpetrators do what they do. I strongly believe we have to take a situational stance here, and look at the different contexts perpetrators move within. From this position flows the first and most central part of my argument, which concerns the way spatial sur-roundings of soldiers influence their behaviour and their morality through their planning and construction, the way they are imagined by the actors involved and the way they are practically used in the context of the Al-Aqsa Intifada. I position my work next to the work of other scholars who have analyzed the Israeli case and who have studied different aspects that influence the behaviour of soldiers. My work thus contributes to this body of literature with the innovative focus on space. Using the concepts of Lefebvre (2007) and Herbert (1997), these influences will be analyzed and I will show how processes of numbing on different levels are shaped within these spaces. In doing this I take theories about space and power and the many theories on factors influencing soldiers' use of violence a step further, connecting them within the context of present-day conflict.

Second, I argue in this work that Israeli soldiers, when recounting about their experiences in the field, use specific discursive strategies to legitimate and normalize their (mis)behaviour. With the help of the work of Cohen (2001) and Bandura (2002) I will analyze this 'soldier talk' to unravel the patterns of denial and moral disengagement used by Israeli conscripts.

CHAPTER 3

CHECKPOINTS, ARRESTS AND PATROLS

Spaces of Occupation

After a while you forget it's a house where someone lives, it becomes your outpost. When you stand guard at the window ... there isn't any furniture in the house; they get everything out to a side room. So, it's not a home anymore.

In this chapter I will discuss the central arenas or spaces within which Israeli soldiers perform their work in the Occupied Palestinian Territories. As I believe the physical surroundings of soldiers have a profound effect on the way they feel and thus act, I will try to understand 'physically' what soldiers go through while working in the OPT. In order to do this I will focus on the characteristics of the spatial surroundings the soldiers work in and their physical circumstances.

These spatial surroundings are, first of all, the checkpoints where many Israeli combat soldiers spend months, if not years, of their service. Apart from the checkpoints, arrests and the so-called 'straw widows' are also important arenas within which Israeli soldiers carry out their work.[8] Here the actual spaces where the soldiers act are the houses of Palestinians that they enter in order to arrest a suspect, carry out a house search or in order to occupy as a temporary military post. These arenas can be physical, actual buildings or constructions like checkpoints, but they can also be activities such as arrests or patrolling that are not bound to a specific physical place, but do involve movement within a specific private or public space. I will look at these spaces and the activities of soldiers within them through the analytical lenses provided for by Lefebvre (2007) and

---

8. This term that is used for a house that has been abandoned by its inhabitants, and that is used by the military for strategic reasons, presumably comes from the term 'grass widow': 'The grass widow is a wife whose husband is away often or for a prolonged period. The origin of this expression comes from the unmarried mother of the 16th century. A child created out of wedlock was assumed to have resulted from a couple's adventures on a bed of grass and not the proper marital bed, hence, grass widow. This can be compared with the German strohwitwe or straw widow'. From www.tribuneindia.com/2004/20040417/windows/roots.htm as accessed on 17 May 2011.

Herbert (1997) about the production of space and spatial practices of control (territoriality).

Policing by Soldiers: Dirty Work

> This is hard work I feel like a guard dog, like the cubes of concrete that surround the checkpoint. They turned us into a front line bunch of fighters, and now we stand at the checkpoint like police and inspect identity cards. Where is the action that we were promised?
>
> (From 'Checkpoint Syndrome', excerpt of poem by Ron-Furer 2003)[9]

Figure 1 Soldiers at work: checking Palestinians moving between one side of the wall to the other (photo: EP)

Before I start to discuss the different spaces soldiers work in, one very central aspect of their work should be highlighted. The work Israeli sol-

9. Translated and published on www.ifamericansknew.org/download/checkpoint_ syndrome.pdf as accessed on 17 May 2011. Ron-Furer's work resulted from his own experiences as a soldier in the OPT and is written in the form of short poems: 'By moving from realistic experiences to surrealistic hallucinations, the text introduces an alternative presentation of the horrible in accordance with the poetic of the extreme, where the borders between sanity and madness are often tested' (Mendelson-Maoz 2005). Because the original work was unavailable and only the translated version could be used, there is a possibility that mistakes have been made in the presentation of the poem.

diers perform in the OPT is not so much classical military work as it is policing work. The excerpt of the poem by Ron-Furer, cited above, gives us an insight into the way this makes soldiers feel. The main tasks of soldiers working within the occupation, as we shall see shortly, consist of guarding, carrying out arrests, manning checkpoints and searching people, cars and houses. Importantly, the intense contact with the civilian population is an aspect of the work that makes it profoundly different from the 'classical' military work of combat operations against hostile enemies. Actual combat, as we shall see further on, is only a small part of the activities for most Israeli combat soldiers in the OPT.

Franke writes about a similar case that is relevant here; Canadian soldiers who were sent out to perform peacekeeping duties in the 1990s. Although Israeli soldiers certainly are not involved in peacekeeping, they are involved in work that is completely different from the work they feel belongs to their identity as combat soldiers. Franke writes that 'if ... soldiers invoke cognitive frames (e.g. warrior) that are ill-suited for a particular assignment (e.g. peacekeeping) morale, motivation, and performance might suffer' (1999: 4).[10] Miller and Moskos made similar observations concerning American troops in Somalia who were sent on a 'humanitarian mission' but who identified with a '"warrior strategy" in which soldiers generalized the behaviour of the gunmen/rioters to all Somalis and treated the entire population as potential enemies' (Miller and Moskos 1995: 618).

As in the above examples, the constabulary activities Israeli soldiers have to carry out do not fit within the identification of soldiers as Israeli combatants. Concerning the First Intifada that began in 1987, Liebes and Blum-Kulka wrote that 'the situation is one in which Israeli soldiers are being called upon to employ means for the repression of civil violence that defy both the behavioural and the moral principles according to which the Israeli army is trained to defend itself against the armed forces of an enemy' (Liebes and Blum-Kulka 1994: 45). This is still true for the situation in the Territories today. Israeli soldiers carry out tasks that are first and foremost policing tasks that do not fit within their understanding of the ideal Israeli soldier as defender of his country.

This constabulary work can be termed 'dirty work', a term coined by Hughes to denote work that is contaminated by a moral, social or physical taint (1958). Work such as prostitution, garbage collection or work in funeral homes can be perceived by the workers themselves and by the public in general as 'dirty'. Soldiering, and especially the kind of soldiering Israeli soldiers face in the OPT, also fits within this list as it is certainly morally tainted and is often seen as boring, hard and uninteresting by

---

10. Article was retrieved online from http://journals.hil.unb.ca/index.php/JCS/article/view/4359/5018 as accessed on 6 September 2012, and page numbers used here are according to that version and may differ from the paper version.

the soldiers themselves. In the words of one soldier a distinction is made between work that is 'sexy' and work that is 'not sexy':

> We would call it 'sexy' or 'not sexy'. 'Sexy' means quiet actions done under cover of night that are worked on a long time. You arrive, do your work and leave. 'Not sexy' is what we did then in the Territories. We felt like labourers. We came, blew up a house and that's it. We felt that they were giving us dirty jobs and a lot of frustration accumulated in the unit.
>
> (quoted in *NRG/Maariv* 2 June 2005)[11]

When telling about their service, Israeli soldiers speak about their work in clear-cut terms of black or dirty work, boredom and routine, except for periods in which this routine is broken and work becomes 'interesting'.

As such, 'dirty work' has its effect on the morale and on the motivation of soldiers to serve. Serving as a combat soldier and defending the state is an ideal for many young people in Israel and the reality of constabulary tasks can, therefore, be disappointing for them. This can enhance the numbing processes described in this work and can, consequently, negatively influence soldiers' behaviour vis-a-vis the Palestinian 'other'.

Checkpoints: Obstruction of Passage

Figure 2 A military post in Hebron (photo: courtesy of Breaking the Silence)

---

11. www.kibush.co.il/show_file.asp?num=3551 as accessed on 30 May 2012.

Human bodies are controlled by predetermined routes overloaded with rail-
ing, barbed wire, electronic fencing, boulders, stone and canvas walls, escala-
tors and one way passages.

                                                                    (Zanger 2005: 42)

Checkpoints in the Occupied Palestinian Territories come in many different shapes and sizes. There are big, permanent checkpoints (that in
recent years have been made to look like international border terminals)
and there are smaller ones with a few soldiers manning the post who
check passing Palestinians randomly or block the road in case of a closure. There are also temporary or 'flying' checkpoints that can be set up
on any road in the OPT to stop suspicious cars or to demonstrate the military presence in the area and deter militants from carrying out attacks.
In this case, only a few soldiers and a jeep are employed to block roads
and check the traffic that comes through. Ben-Ari, Maymon, Gazit and
Shatzberg speak of five different forms of checkpoints: the 'encirclement
checkpoints', 'flying checkpoints', 'closure checkpoints', 'back-to-back
checkpoints' and finally the gates along the security barrier (Ben-Ari
et al. 2004). At the time of writing there were approximately twenty-
seven permanent checkpoints manned by Israeli soldiers in the OPT not
including the twenty-six checkpoints along the Green Line.[12] In addition,
there a few dozen flying or temporary checkpoints a week in the West
Bank and hundreds of physical obstructions that block off roads and
paths leading into villages and cities.[13]

Checkpoints, or Are They …

Technically speaking, checkpoints are, as the name has it, points for
checking; people and goods are examined by soldiers to make sure that
no explosives or weapons are taken from one side of the checkpoint to the
other. Furthermore, identity cards are checked to make sure that no one
passes through without a permit. From the point of view of the Israeli military and the political establishment, checkpoints are necessary in the fight
against terrorism because they prevent militants or terrorists from moving
within the Territories and especially from exiting into Israel. In Lefebvre's
terms, this can be described as a representation of space (2007); space
is designed as an impersonal place where certain activities take place as
efficiently as possible. No attention is given to the actual spatial practice
of the checkpoint, which I will discuss later, or the relationship between
the different agents (soldiers and Palestinians).

---

12. The Green Line refers to the 1949 armistice line and separates Israel from the
    OPT. The wall that is being built between both territories coincides with this line
    in a few places but more often than not reaches deep into Palestinian lands.
13. Data B'Tselem www.btselem.org/freedom_of_movement/checkpoints as accessed
    on 30 May 2012.

The causal relationship implied by Israeli policy, between Israeli security and the checkpoints in the OPT, has been questioned and in recent years many big checkpoints have been dismantled.[14] A report by twelve retired generals from the IDF that was sent to Minister of Defence Ehud Barak claims that dismantling the checkpoints in the Territories would actually serve Israel's security better.[15] The letter claims that the severe restrictions the checkpoints pose for the Palestinian population only increase hatred, thus heightening the chances of more terrorist activity. Many checkpoints were set up with a specific purpose (such as diminishing or stopping a potential threat) but lost their original role many years ago. One member of the team of generals is quoted by a UN news source as saying: 'I founded the Qalandia checkpoint years ago as a flying security checkpoint for a specific reason ... to prevent a specific attack we had intelligence on ... that checkpoint hasn't been removed years later'.[16]

Figure 3 Small checkpoint in the OPT (photo: EP)

14. See for example the following article www.haaretz.com/print-edition/news/idf-to-remove-major-west-bank-checkpoint-to-enable-palestinian-movement-1.342612 as accessed on 30 May 2012.
15. See article on the report on www.usatoday.com/news/world/2008-02-13-3462899240_x.htm as accessed on 17 May 2011.
16. Quoted in http://files.tikkun.org/current/article.php?story=20080319120835772 as accessed on 9 July 2008.

In order to travel through different areas within the OPT, Palestinians need a permit. These permits are distributed by the DCO (District Coordination Office) of the IDF. Most Palestinians have to pass checkpoints daily to get to work, to school, to visit family members, to go shopping or to see a doctor. Rules on who is allowed to pass the checkpoint, and who is not, change from day to day and depend on orders from either the higher echelons of the military or from lower commanders in the field. The arbitrariness of commands and the implementation of rules is typical for the situation in the OPT since the outbreak of the Al-Aqsa Intifada, as Ben-Ari, Lerer, Ben-Shalom and Vainer have observed in their detailed study of this conflict (Ben-Ari et al. 2010: 41–42).

Hammami, invoking the 'spatial practices' or real experienced space as found in Lefebvre's work (2007), describes the web of checkpoints in the OPT:

> [A]s a macro-structure, the more than 400 checkpoints and roadblocks constitute a spatial regime of incarceration that has delivered more than 50% of the population into poverty and rendered a quarter of them workless. While on the micro level of everyday interaction they constitute the most visceral experience of our relationship of inequality with Israel, and a profound reminder of our status as stateless people.
>
> (Hammami 2006: 4)

Through Hammami's words the far-reaching implications of the checkpoints on the life of the Palestinian population become all the more clear.

Likewise, Doumani reminds us in her description of the situation around the city of Nablus, that the name checkpoint is actually a misleading one:

> [T]he military points in Hawara and Bayt Eba are more like permanent border crossings than temporary roadblocks. At both crossings, large areas have been levelled to make way for complex security procedures that control the flow of traffic: pedestrian and car lanes, fortified bunkers, guard towers bristling with heavy machineguns and shrouded with camouflage netting, fences and barriers.
>
> (Doumani 2004: 37)

In the following quotation, Nir,[17] a commander from the Nahal Brigade and a kibbutz member,[18, 19] explains the work at a checkpoint during a curfew and a closure:

---

17. All names are pseudonyms in order to protect the privacy of the informants.
18. A *kibbutz* is an agricultural settlement, usually based on socialist ideals brought to Israel from the former Soviet Union with Jewish immigrants in the 1940s.
19. The Nahal Brigade is a brigade within which soldiers can combine agricultural or social work with their military service. Many of its members (especially from Brigade 50) are from *Kibbutzim* or *Moshavim*.

> If there was a closure or curfew, it's hard [the work at the checkpoint]. You prevent everyone from getting out ... when there is a curfew they [the Palestinians], don't get out of their houses, with a closure they don't get out of the village, they have to stay in their village. There is no passing between the villages, from Hebron there is no passing to Halhul, and from Halhul to ... these passages are closed ... there is no traffic between the villages.

A checkpoint could be seen as an 'in-between' space, a 'border space' separating two entities, two countries or two people. A point of passage that lets you pass from one space to another or, as Zanger describes it: '[T]he checkpoint functions as the regulator of control and rule: the mechanism of surveillance and control operates by spatial, ideological, and linguistic means, which include a ritual of such repetitive acts as identification, obedience, reward and punishment' (Zanger 2005: 38).

In the OPT the checkpoint is indeed not just a passing point. It is a mechanism separating two unequal entities and it is a point of obstruction where one group is dominant and in total control over the other, subordinate group, a character of asymmetrical conflict. The checkpoint in the OPT is not an 'in-between' space that does not really belong to this or that side; it is an Israeli 'micro-space' either within the larger Palestinian space or along the border between Israeli and Palestinian lands. The checkpoints Israeli soldiers man often separate one Palestinian area from another and do not, as is often believed, solely separate Palestinian from Israeli territory. Palestinian cities are separated from the villages around them and from other cities in their vicinity. Travelling between cities within the OPT has become a difficult if not impossible endeavour for most Palestinians. Hammami gives the view from the Palestinian side when she writes: '[T] here is a collective understanding that the checkpoints are there to stop life, to destroy livelihoods and education and ultimately defeat the will of a nation' (Hammami 2006: 24). As the soldier mentions in the quotation above, sometimes when orders for a closure are given, whole villages or cities are isolated from the outside world. These facts make the checkpoints in the OPT points of friction rather than points of passage (Ben-Ari et al. 2004).

Ethnography of the Checkpoint Arena

To get 'a feel' for this important arena that Israeli soldiers work in, I will present a short ethnography of the Qalandia checkpoint located next to the Palestinian city of Ramallah, close to Jerusalem. This will give us a better understanding of the spaces soldiers work within. In recent years this particular checkpoint was transformed from a busy, noisy, open-air checkpoint to a full-blown terminal with benches for the waiting crowds, sophisticated security measures, cameras, turnstiles and even a parking area. On the website of the Ministry of Foreign Affairs the following explanation for this change was given:

[N]ew checkpoint facilities have been opened to enable speedy and efficient security checks in a minimum of time. This is intended to ease the lives of Palestinian residents who aren't involved in bringing terrorism to Israel. ... The improved crossings have been erected both at places which did and did not previously have checkpoints, and were placed after examining where it would be possible to preserve and even improve the lives of the Palestinians using them.[20]

This idea and the official discourse describing a new kind of checkpoint can be categorized as a representation of space (Lefebvre 2007). It has been planned with a 'business-like' idea of how a checkpoint should run smoothly and efficiently, without considering the power relations at play for example, and the humiliation of Palestinians who are forced to be checked.

The explanation on the ministry's website is clearly geared towards the international community and it is most likely an effort to improve the image of the IDF in that community's eyes. While it may be that these terminals improve the speed of the flow of people going through at times, it is very likely that these changes were made to create more permanent structures and 'facts on the ground', making it possible for the Israeli military to have tighter control over the Palestinian population. (See also, in regard to this, the comment about the Qalandia checkpoint by the above quoted general.)

When visiting Qalandia in the spring of 2006, after the reconstruction of the checkpoint, men, women and children were still standing in long lines waiting for the soldiers to let them through so that they could carry on with their daily activities. Besides its new look, a new concept was implemented regarding the proximity of soldiers and Palestinians – a complete physical separation between both was created.

At the old checkpoint, soldiers would stand outside under a tin roof behind piles of sandbags that served as a security measure. In this setup, the soldiers were in direct contact with the passing Palestinians, checking their bodies, bags, IDs and other possessions manually. At the new checkpoint, soldiers sit behind bulletproof glass, speak only through an intercom and manage the stream of passing Palestinians from a distance. When IDs or permits have to be shown, they are put in a metal drawer that is pulled inwards by the soldiers for inspection. The Palestinian 'passengers' put their bags through the X-ray machines and walk through a metal detector just like at any border crossing at an air, land or sea 'port' between two countries. As mentioned before, this comparison is no coincidence as such checkpoints are erected as permanent border crossings, creating 'facts on the ground'.

---

20. www.mfa.gov.il/MFA/Government/Communiques/2005/New+terminals+at+ch eckpoints+in+West+Bank+6-Jul-2005.htm as accessed on 17 May 2011.

Figure 4 Qalandia checkpoint, new style (photo: EP)

Figure 5 Qalandia checkpoint, new style (photo: EP)

The (in)famous wall or, as the official Israeli state discourse has it, the security barrier, has been built right next to the checkpoint, making the checkpoint the main entry point to Jerusalem from Ramallah. The parking spaces beside the new terminal are unused as no one can reach the checkpoint by car. Taxis take their passengers to a point some 200 metres from the entrance, from where one has to walk to the terminal. After passing, one can find taxis on the other side, again after walking about 200 metres. To enter and exit the checkpoint, one has to pass through metal turnstiles, which makes it very hard to carry large objects such as suitcases and children's strollers as these do not fit through. For this reason children are carried in their mother's arms through most checkpoints in the OPT.

When arriving at Qalandia on that Spring day in April, the checkpoint seemed to have been abandoned by soldiers. The doors were closed and a few dozen Palestinians were stuck between two one-way passages and could not get out. One daring youth climbed over the metal turnstile and squeezed through a small space to get to the other side.

After a closer look, however, it became clear that behind the dark glass a few soldiers were actually present and they, after the pleading of some Israelis,[21] released the turnstile so people could go through. The reason for the temporary closure of the checkpoint was unclear and was not explained by the soldiers behind the bulletproof glass either because they did not have a clear answer or because of the difficulty of communicating through the glass.

After going through the checkpoint to the Palestinian side, which was fairly easy as the pedestrians moving in this direction were hardly checked, the way back to the Israeli side commenced. This turned out to be much more difficult. Again, the passage was blocked and no one could go through. Men and women stood in different lines, pushing one another. Women with crying children in their arms did their best to go through as fast as possible, receiving help from others who were standing in line. The crowds were harshly ordered around by the soldiers through the intercom system. The soldiers did not come outside of their isolated cabin and their faces remained anonymous. Only after about twenty minutes the passage was opened; one by one people could walk through the metal turnstile and through the different checking mechanisms (such as the metal detector and the X-ray machine) towards the other side.

During another visit in February, the rain turned the whole area around the checkpoint into a muddy pool. It was cold in the terminal, people were shouting, children were crying, there was pushing and shoving and faces were angry with frustration. The waiting area smelled of damp clothes and crowds.

---

21. Members of the Coalition of Women for Peace.

Figure 6 Qalandia checkpoint (photo: EP)

The bulletproof glass behind which the Israeli soldiers sit and work at this checkpoint protects them, perhaps unintentionally, from direct confrontation with these hardships, from seeing the crowds, from feeling the cold and from hearing the shouts of frustration. This checkpoint is, however, one of the exceptions. Most of the smaller checkpoints that Israeli soldiers man give them no protection from sensing 'the other', feeling the heat or the cold, smelling the crowds and hearing the complaints and the pleas. Both situations (the one where soldiers and Palestinians are separated and the one where a close encounter takes place between both parties) influence the soldiers' behaviour in their own way as we shall see further on.

Arrests and 'Straw Widows': Entering the Private Palestinian Domain

The second main arena or space of Israeli soldiers' work that I would like to discuss here is in fact a very private Palestinian domain – the private houses of Palestinian citizens. Private houses are entered to carry out arrests and in order to occupy these houses for a longer period of time as temporary military posts. I will divide the description of this space in two parts: arrests and 'straw widows', as both forms of 'territoriality' (Sacks as used by Herbert 1997) by soldiers have different characteristics and influence the soldiers differently.

Figure 7 Soldiers with an arrestee in a Palestinian building (photo: courtesy of Breaking the Silence)

Arrests

> [T]hese people never knew what hit them. We busted in when they were sleeping. Scared the living shit out of them. Half a dozen little kids, a woman in traditional black Arabic clothing, and the target individual, all sleeping on the ground in the outdoor part of the house. The kids were screaming in fear and crying and so was the lady.

> (Buzzell 2005: 239)[22]

After intelligence information is received about a wanted individual, one or more teams of soldiers are sent off to carry out the arrest. There are different ways of carrying out an arrest, but in general they take place at night and begin with a knock on the door. When the family opens the door, the women and children are separated from the men and from amongst the men the suspect is identified.[23] The suspect is then taken to the General Security Service (Shabak) for questioning.

---

22. In his book *My War: Killing Time in Iraq*, American soldier Colby Buzzell (2005) tells about his experiences as a serviceman in Iraq.
23. While there probably have been arrests of women, the great majority of arrest operations concern men. During my interviews I did not come across any arrests of women.

Arrest operations are either planned weeks in advance by elite combat units or are organized at the spur of the moment when there is a 'ticking bomb' involved, i.e. information on a terror attack that is going to be carried out in the very near future. Arrests, furthermore, involve different units, all with their own specialties. Some units give security backup around the house of the wanted individual while others enter the house to carry out the actual arrest.

Doron, a member of a *kibbutz* in central Israel who served as a squad commander in a paratroopers unit, performed many night nightly arrests, which became a completely routine experience for him. He relates about the way arrests were organized:

> It is like, in the evening the information arrives [about] what is going to happen that evening. Then the company commander chooses to what platoon he gives the assignment ... the platoon commander divides the crews, everyone with its own mission, there are those that secure the house, those that go into the house, some that do searches, some that don't. And then usually you go to an Israeli settlement,[24] next to the city, you go make a model, you get photos of the house and all.

> Usually it's really routine; from the moment you get in the house, little contact as possible with the family, you take the family, there is a person that is responsible for it, you put everyone in the bedroom or the living room, you don't let them see what you are doing in the house. You tell them to sit still, they also know it very well, like us, the Arabs,[25] they know if they sit still nothing happens, the mother always starts to cry over her child, 'leave him alone' and all, till it ends and then we leave them.

From both descriptions the routine of the operation becomes very clear. Entering a Palestinian house becomes a natural thing; I will discuss shortly how such normalization takes place. The power soldiers have over the Palestinians also becomes very clear here. As we will see in the case of 'straw widows' as well, soldiers exercise territoriality over these Palestinian houses. They take complete control over a space, leaving the inhabitants in this case, completely powerless. Going further than in Herbert's description of policemen in Los Angeles controlling public space, these soldiers control private space and transform it into a military space. This point will be discussed later after also looking at the spatial practices of soldiers in 'straw widows'.

---

24. By 'Israeli settlement' Doron means one of the Jewish settlements within the OPT.
25. Within Israel the term 'Arab' is usually used for Palestinians who are Israeli citizens and who live inside the 'Green Line' while the term 'Palestinian' is used for the inhabitants of the OPT in an attempt to create the appearance of two different nations. Appreciating the way people actually identify themselves, Rabinowitz has used the term 'Palestinian citizens of Israel' (2001).

Straw Widows

Besides going into Palestinian houses for very short periods of time to arrest a suspect, Israeli soldiers also occupy Palestinian houses, which then become 'straw widows', for strategic purposes. For days, weeks or months on end, a military unit can stay within such a house, which is (partly) converted into a military post. The Palestinian family living in the house is usually moved to one floor or even one room in the house, depending on the space available, and is guarded at all times by a soldier. The family's movement within the house and outside of it is severely restricted by the presence of Israeli soldiers in their home. Again, Doron relates about his experience of such operations:

> Then you stay there, there are soldiers, there is a shift that is in charge of the family, they don't look out to the street, for 24 hours; 3 hours you look out for the family, 3 hours you look out, then you sleep. The family stays in a closed room, until you leave. You give them water, someone that has to go to the toilet, you go with them, he gets in the toilet, you take him back, they are imprisoned until you leave. (Q: 'Isn't there a chance they will get the information [about the Israeli soldiers being in their house] to others?') That's the thing, you leave them, you lock them, you take their telephones, mobile phones, you close the windows, usually you take them to a room without windows, they are isolated, like that.

Figure 8 'Straw widow' in Hebron (photo: EP)

Again we see the enormous amount of power soldiers have over the Palestinians living in the houses they occupy. Palestinians become power-less within their own private space that is completely controlled by Israeli forces.

Yariv, another *kibbutz* member who served in the elite unit of the Nahal Brigade, comes from what he calls a leftist home and is critical of the activities of the Israeli military in the OPT.[26] When speaking about his experiences in 'straw widows' he shows some negative emotions. However, note that these negative emotions concern him and not so much the inhabitants in the house he invades:

> You have a thing that is called 'straw widow' in the military, that's to be in an Arab house for a few days, that was horrible, I remember it was ... (Q: 'What happens exactly?') You get inside the house; you move the whole family to a room of their own. (Q: 'Do they know in advance that you are coming?') No, they don't know in advance. You get into the house, their house has an advantage for us like a good observation point, and the family goes into one room, someone watches the family ... but you don't touch their things.

Figure 9 'Straw widow' in Hebron (photo: EP)

---

26. When soldiers specifically state their political orientation in connection to the way they act and make decisions, this orientation is mentioned. This type of information was volunteered and in no way solicited.

Entering the Private Domain

Central to the activity of arrests or the occupation of a Palestinian house for a longer period of time is the very act of the military entering a private Palestinian home. In the case of a 'straw widow', this home is even converted into a military post. The physical closeness to the private lives of Palestinians and the sensory experience of seeing, hearing, feeling and smelling are of importance here. The soldiers enter a different, sometimes hostile, but also very personal space.

Soldiers, as said before, take over complete control over this space. I use Lefebvre's ideas here, as I believe soldiers produce a military space through their spatial practices; they take furniture out of the house, they lock the inhabitants into one room and they make as little contact with the Palestinians as possible. In this way they can imagine the space to be a military one and not a domestic one, where they find their place, as soldiers, in comfort. Theirs is an ultimate power, not only controlling space, but transforming a domestic space for their own use, leaving the original inhabitants completely powerless.

The contrast between military bodies and the private houses they enter becomes clear when we look at pictures taken by Israeli soldiers. Soldiers everywhere take pictures of the places they have been to and of the things they have seen and done. These can be innocent images of landscapes or smiling comrades. However, as photos of prisoners taken by American and British soldiers in Iraq have shown us, they can also be horrifying. Israeli soldiers like to take pictures of themselves during their military service, especially today with digital cameras and smartphones within arm's reach. They photograph their activities, including those within the private homes of Palestinians. These pictures can give us some insights into the encounter between the military and the private domain for operations involving arrest or occupation ('straw widows'). We can, for example, see soldiers in full combat dress (including boots) on soft, homely couches, sitting in a family's living room.

Even if they are careful, as some soldiers wanted to assure me of, they will eventually and inevitably disturb the house, opening closets and drawers, moving furniture and touching the personal belongings of the family. In many instances, the personal belongings of the Palestinian families are even used by the soldiers, for example mattresses and carpets to sleep on during longer stays. Soldiers are also known to have used TV sets at times, as the following quote from a soldier interviewed by Breaking the Silence shows:

> We were in the middle of a house-searching operation in the refugee camp, when we entered one of the houses, evacuated the family into one room, according to procedure, and searched the house. By the way – as we entered, the family was watching the soccer world-cup finals and left the TV on. We were tempted and sat to watch the game. Gradually, everybody joined, the

Figure 10 Soldiers watching football in a Palestinian house (photo: courtesy of Breaking the Silence)

Figure 11 Military unit inside Palestinian house (photo: courtesy of Breaking the Silence)

whole unit, crowded in front of the TV – including the platoon's vice-commander – and watched the game. Meanwhile the family waited in the room we put them into earlier.
(BS maltreatment)

If we can imagine the atmosphere in a Palestinian house during an arrest or a search we can probably sense the fear and frustration of the residents. This description of a military operation by a Palestinian writer is telling:

> The residents of each apartment building are rounded up at gunpoint and stuffed into a single room on the ground floor. The scene is disconcerting: men in their pyjamas ill at ease in someone else's home; children crying, whining, or peeing in their pants; women trying to be useful but hardly able even to make their way across the jam-packed room; awkward lines for a single bathroom; furtive eyes on the door locked from the outset and guarded by Israeli soldiers; a young girl crying quietly in a corner; general panic if anyone tries to look out the window.

(Doumani 2004: 42–3)

The soldier is, in reality, a military body entering the ultimate personal space of a family home. Sensory experiences, such as sight, smell and noise intensify and concretize the surroundings of the soldiers. They also mark the differences between the soldiers as Israeli citizens and the Palestinian civilians who live in such different circumstances, for example through the sight and smell of a house and its inhabitants.

However, for many soldiers the situation is not as unnatural or abnormal as one might expect. Looking back at the quote that introduced this chapter, it is interesting to note that the soldier quoted describes how the personal space of the home is militarized and depersonalized by the entrance of the soldiers and by the taking out of all the furniture. It seems to make the stay of the soldiers inside the houses easier when they can think of the space as military and not as private. We could say that representational space (Lefebvre 2007), where space is imagined, is invoked here as soldiers seem to imagine the space as being different than it is in reality. Imagining it as a military space instead of a private space helps them to normalize their experience and suppress uncomfortable feelings.

> (Q: 'Would you feel uncomfortable when entering a Palestinian house?') No, it was very normal for me. Very much normal to get into a house of a wanted man, I didn't give it any thought. But with time, you start seeing how they live, the way they lead their lives, it's in the dumps. Simply horrible. You start to be indifferent, just like with the attrition [*shkhika*] of the operation, you get into a house, there are like twenty people in a house of 1.5 rooms, the kitchen, for a month no one has done the dishes, and everyone sleeps on the floor, and it's disgusting, smelly, every time it disgusts you anew, but you don't pay attention

to it too much, you see it, you take it in, it pops up in your head, it doesn't hurt the operation, you go on as usual.

Doron, who was cited before and who emphasized his leftist, political orientation, relates time and again of how this orientation influenced his behaviour towards Palestinians. Here he tells about how he sees the suffering of the Palestinians from up close every time he enters their homes. However, as he is tied up in the operation, he does not let himself be influenced by their hardships: 'you see it, you take it in ... it doesn't hurt the operation'. The situation around him is normalized and he doesn't pay attention to it after a while. Entering a private Palestinian house becomes a 'normal' activity. He does something similar to what American soldier Hartley did in Iraq: 'I decided to check my politeness at the door and search for the weapons that these guys were trying to kill us with, like I was fucking supposed to. I still feel bad ... ' (Hartley 2006: 99).

Some soldiers, however, stated that they felt somewhat uncomfortable with their presence in this private space. Shmuel, a *kibbutz* member who was to his surprise drafted to the Givati Brigade where being from a socialist *kibbutz* background is an exception, tells of how he would feel when entering a Palestinian house: 'Listen it's not nice, a lot of times, that is to say, I felt like that, not many people felt like that, but I felt that it's not nice [*lo na'im*] you go into the house of simple people that didn't do anything'.

However, as Shmuel mentions here, not many soldiers felt the same and as we can make out from the other examples for most of the others the personal space of a home had been completely militarized and turned into their work arena. Hence their work within it was normalized as 'just' military work.

Patrolling

A third work arena that Israeli soldiers act within is not so much a place as an activity: the patrols soldiers carry out. These patrols can be carried out on foot but are mostly done with military vehicles. Roads around Jewish settlements and Palestinian cities or villages are patrolled and soldiers frequently enter Palestinian cities to patrol the streets.

Patrols, from the point of view of the military, are carried out for security purposes; Jewish settlements within the OPT are secured by patrolling the roads around them – suspicious people are apprehended and curfews within cities are upheld by patrolling the streets. Another important reason for these patrols, especially those undertaken within cities, is described by soldiers as 'showing presence'. In this way the Israeli military shows the militants that are hiding that it is present and that it is ready for action if needed.

'Showing presence' represents the basic rationale of many activities of the IDF within the OPT; temporary checkpoints and 'blank' shooting at walls are, for example, also seen as activities aimed at the confirmation of the presence and power of the IDF. Palestinian space is then not only occupied horizontally as it were, but also vertically, to include as much of the space as possible and demonstrate the Israeli's state power.

A staff sergeant tells the story of a nightly patrol he carried out in the city of Nablus:

> There were operations titled 'Looking for Trouble'. What does 'Looking for Trouble' mean? It means going on a patrol, touring the *Kasbah*,[27] hope someone will shoot at us, and that we get into combat. 'Looking For Trouble' is the name the guys gave it ... Night patrol in the *Kasbah* in Nablus. Usually the reason for those patrols was to try to get into some combat, and to show our presence.

> (BS fire opening)

Another important characteristic of patrolling is that the soldiers never really know what will happen and who they will meet during their rounds. This uncertainty combined with being vulnerable, especially when patrolling on foot, can make soldiers insecure and this in turn can influence their behaviour.

However, soldiers on patrols are also much freer in their movements than, for example, when they are working at a checkpoint. Often patrolling can be boring and soldiers will try to find things to do to pass the time, such as randomly searching people they do not need to search. Patrolling is territorializing Palestinian space in yet another way. Soldiers show their power and potential (for violence) in order to control the Palestinians and their movements within this space.

Conclusion

If we want to understand soldiers' behaviour and get closer to grasping their moralities we need to gain insights into the way soldiers are affected by their spatial surroundings and how this in the end influences their (moral) behaviour. In this chapter the 'scene' was set for this work and the most central working arenas (or moral regions) of Israeli soldiers in the OPT were discussed: checkpoints, arrests, 'straw widows' and patrolling. The checkpoints, static places where soldiers were often in direct contact with the Palestinians, the arrests and 'straw widows', during which they actually entered the private Palestinian domain, and the patrolling of the

---

27. *Kasbah* originally comes from the term for Islamic city or fortress (http://en.wikipedia.org/wiki/Kasbah as accessed 17 May 2011); often the centre of an Arab city in the OPT is called the *Kasbah*.

Palestinian streets all have their own characteristics and ways in which soldiers use spatial practices to control these arenas.

This power relation is crucial here. At the checkpoints we saw that distance was, when possible, kept from the Palestinians whose movement through the checkpoint completely depended on the soldiers. The planning of the checkpoint as efficient point of passage is a clear example of Lefebvre's representation of place. In this chapter I tried to fill the void of this use with the actual spatial practices of this space. Within the private space of Palestinians, soldiers used militarizing techniques to transfer such space into a space they, as soldiers, could feel 'at home' in. Families were put away into secured rooms and as little contact as possible was made with them. Complete control was established over these private spaces.

In the next chapter the operational dynamics of these spaces described here will be analyzed further. Issues such as power, already featured here, and routine will be discussed to show how these concepts are connected to the (moral) behaviour of the soldiers in the Occupied Palestinian Territories.

CHAPTER 4

PERFORMING AS OCCUPIERS
Operational Dynamics

A child arrives, you tell him 'Listen, I'll let you pass now, but do me a favour and go home', and five minutes later he's back. Then you tell him, 'Listen here, you said you'd go, now get lost', and two months later, I think it's enough, you don't need a year, a month is enough, a week is enough for you to get fed up with this child and with all these people, you are on eight-hour guard duty, and you are so tired, and so bummed, and so burnt out and you don't give a fuck about any of this shit, and then a person comes, and you don't care if he's old, if he's a man, a woman, an adult, a kid, you don't give a damn what species, race, or colour he is, he arrives and you tell him 'La, ruh `al beit' [No, go home]. You tell him 'Turn around and go home'. 'I'm not interested in any excuses; I'm not interested in anything. You want to buy vegetables? What do I care about your vegetables? There's a curfew. Period. You don't move. Your house is in the other direction? I don't care, find another way, you can't pass from here'.

(BS Hebron)

The Israeli soldier quoted above describes a process he went through while serving at a checkpoint in the OPT. With time, he got more and more impatient with the Palestinians who came through the checkpoint where he worked, which resulted in an indifference towards their pleas and, eventually, in him shouting at them. Several elements that contributed to this process are mentioned: long hours of work at the checkpoint, fatigue, feeling burnt out and frustration.

In this chapter I will look more closely at the performance of soldiers within the work spaces described before. I will highlight a few central properties that characterize soldiering within an occupied space. These properties of soldiering also deeply influence the kind of work soldiers do and the way it makes them feel and react to their surroundings. The work in all the arenas described share these properties, they are, however, experienced and materialized differently within each arena. First, I will discuss the routine that comes up again and again in interviews with soldiers. This will be followed by discussing the IDF's Operation Defensive Shield, carried out in 2002 as a case study. This operation took place as a reaction to a series of suicide bombings in Israel; almost all the major Palestinian cities were invaded by the Israeli military and it was an important formative experience for many of the Israeli soldiers who were involved in it. Precisely because of its extraordinary features outside of normality, it can help us grasp the routine Israeli soldiers experience in their daily work within the OPT and what happens when they break out of this. Third, I will look more closely at the issue of power and the way it materializes within the work of soldiers. Lastly, I will discuss the issue of distance and proximity within the spaces soldiers work in. All these central properties then are very influential for the behaviour of soldiers, as I will show, and represent an important factor in their moral decision making.

Routine

One of the most important characteristics of the work in all of the arenas discussed in the last chapter is the sense of routine soldiers get into once they have experienced the operations a few times. Even during arrests, where more dynamics are at play and more tension is felt, soldiers feel they are working a routine. This routine, however, takes shape differently in each arena.

Hours at the Checkpoint

The long hours and the limited periods of rest in between shifts make work at the checkpoint very hard in the experience of most of the soldiers; some units do the same work with the same hours (for example, four or eight hours work and then four or eight hours rest) for months on end. These are usually the regular combat units, not the special units that extensively train for an operation, go into the OPT, carry out their tasks and get out of the OPT again.

Regular combat soldiers from the infantry, for example, can find themselves working at the same checkpoint for long periods of time. The routine at the checkpoint is one of boredom, monotonous views (the same trees, the same rocks), monotonous work (checking IDs, asking the same questions over and over again, getting the same answers) and the same set daily programme (eight hours at the checkpoint, two hours training, six hours rest, for example). This staff sergeant conveys this well:

> And the routine: eight/eight. That non-realistic legend of eight hours at the checkpoint and eight hours resting – in reality this is nine hours at the post and five resting. That's how it is. And you have briefings and you have that ... A soldier begins to wear out. He gets to the checkpoint and loses his patience.
>
> (BS 1001)

Although different in its objectives, the long hours at the checkpoints can be perhaps compared to the hours spent by soldiers on guard duty. Guard duty can be done at a base, an outpost or a settlement amongst other places. Yoel, a squad commander, describes the routine of soldiers on guard duty and sympathizes with the hardship they undergo:

> It wears you out; you can't deal with such a thing. Can you imagine that you are at this place for a year and that all you do is to get up in the morning, get up to guard, 8 hours, get down, do the dishes and tasks, etc., sleep for 4 hours, and go up for 8. Every 18 days you have 3 days you can rest, and you want to do as much as possible so you don't sleep and then you go back. ... You can't deal with it, they [the soldiers] aren't robots.

A few important themes are linked here to the experience of routine; losing one's patience, the wearing out of soldiers and the feeling that it is impossible for soldiers to work within such a hard routine. I will discuss in the next chapter how these aspects of routine work can cause processes of numbing in the soldiers. Important is to notice here the hardship that comes with the endless repetition of specific jobs, such as the case in work in the OPT.

When there is no 'action' at the checkpoint, other ways to pass the time are sought after. Soldiers, as is often emphasized by their commanders, will be interested in any topic that is not connected to their work at the checkpoint. If there are no special operations to break their routine, they will try to pass the time by talking about any topic that eighteen to twenty-one-year-old young men would talk about: girls, music, movies, but also questions like: 'When are we going home?' and 'How long till the end of the shift?' Eviatar, a former company commander in the artillery brigade, immediately admitted that his soldiers loved to talk about anything that was not their job:

> For sure, what mostly interests them is what is not happening at the checkpoint. They want to know what happened yesterday in the other company, what did his girlfriend say to him, who is the new girl he is going out with etc. etc. That interests them much more. That can also be a reason that they have less attention for the situation with the [Palestinian] civilians. It interests them when lunch is coming, why the next shift is late, in short everything that is not connected to the checkpoint interests them.

Routine Arrest

Even though arrests involve more 'action' than the monotonous work at the checkpoint, a routine sets in just the same.

> To tell the truth, most are pretty much complacent it's also because of the attrition [*shkhika*], if you do an arrest every night for two years, the same

things, sometimes 2 or 3 times a night the same thing, there is no time for models [extensive preparation], there is no time, the moment you put your head on the pillow ... Go, there is someone ready, tomorrow he'll carry out an attack so you have to go and get him. So there is this *shkhika*, and complacency, that people get into, but I remember myself every time I went into those refugee camps you become completely alert, it's not fear, it's that you know there are armed people, you get into their house, their area, you know you're in a less advanced position, even though you are the military, if something happens ... there is this tension, but with time people get complacent. (Q: 'Does it become routine?') It's completely a routine.

Doron, who is quoted here and who served in a unit that specialized in arrest operations, conveys how carrying out two or three arrests every night became routine for the soldiers. They performed their duty, carried out the operation as they were supposed to and stayed alert at all times. However, the activities are the same every time and complacency sets in, especially after one has been carrying out such operations for a while. This routine, as we shall see later, contributes to a numbing process that soldiers undergo. It, furthermore, shows how such operations are normalized in the minds of soldiers as 'just' another military operation.

Morale and 'Real Action'

As already mentioned in Chapter 2 when discussing the concept of 'dirty work', soldiers tend to wait for 'real action' to break away from the routine of their everyday activities. Ron-Furer gives a good example of this in the poetic memoirs of his service in the OPT:

We were on a patrol duty. We got a signal over the radio: 'a suspicious figure in segment 512'. We turned the jeep around and drove there at full speed. We are usually quite stressed because at noon there is not much going on. But a suspicious figure walking about like that in daylight – we knew that it meant there would be some action.

(from 'Checkpoint Syndrome', Ron-Furer 2003)[28]

In Winslow's work on Canadian soldiers in Somalia, similar emotions were seen. One of her informants said: '[A] peace-making mission in Somalia finally offered an opportunity for some gung-ho members of the CAR to prove themselves in battle'[29] (Winslow 1997: 24). Soldiers thus seem to wait for action in order to show 'what they can do' as combat soldiers. Without it, their morale can drop and disillusionment

---

28. Translated and published on www.ifamericansknew.org/download/checkpoint_syndrome.pdf as accessed on 18 June 2008, see furthermore Footnote 9.
29. Canadian Airborne Regiment.

sets in, as was noted by Miller and Moskos amongst American troops
(1995).

> The 'action' is what happens in between, you go to do a checkpoint and sud-
> denly they shoot on you from a house in Jenin. Then you shoot back, and you
> chase him and you don't have time to call anyone so only those who are there
> ... you go back wasted but the soldiers are in ecstasy [*teruf*] they talk about
> it and they are happy something happened. There is cohesion [*gibush*] of a
> few soldiers, they never trained together for it,[30] but did it the whole day. It
> sounds weird now, but then it was a feeling, I don't know ...

In this quote, Asaf, a kibbutz member and former squad commander
from the Golani Brigade, makes a clear connection between 'action',
the breaking of routine and feelings of cohesion within a military unit
or, as in the example he gives, between a few soldiers not familiar with
each other (see Ben-Shalom et al. 2005 for more on 'swift trust' and ad
hoc operating units). The 'action' and excitement seems to bring these
soldiers together and enhances their group solidarity.

The monotony of the work and the routine are also related to the
question of morale; soldiers feel that their job is not a heroic one and
do not feel really connected to their mission within the OPT, something
touched upon before when discussing policing tasks and dirty work.
Breaking the routine, then, is something many soldiers seem to wait
for; when a bomb is found at a checkpoint, everyone becomes alert
again and morale is high. When a unit gets to be part of special, high-
profile operations, this is reason for enthusiasm. As I wrote earlier,
many soldiers feel that the moment they get to experience 'real' action,
as opposed to policing tasks, such as standing at checkpoints and
patrolling the streets, they are finally doing what they were trained for.
Soldiers, especially the younger ones, seem to be keen for 'real' combat.

Looking at the way Israeli youth is educated and how it is brought
up in a way that idealizes combat service, this may come as no surprise.
There is a strong dissonance between the way soldiers and young Israelis
in general are socialized to become combatants and the reality of their
military service. Omer, at the time of the interview just released from
military service, had served in an elite paratrooper unit. He vividly
remembered the emotions of the soldiers when going into the Territories
at the beginning of their service:

---

30. *Gibush* means cohesion. In this context we can use Ben-Ari's definition in which
    the end product of *gibush* 'are motivated individuals who want to be together
    and a tightly knit military unit characterized by egalitarianism, solidarity, and
    strong boundaries and therefore capable of successfully carrying out missions'
    (Ben-Ari 1998: 99).

When you're in the 'basic training' [*maslul*] and they tell you to do an operation in the Territories, you are really happy, you are done with training, you
want to really see, to do something with all these trainings. [When] you are
a fighter, after the track and everything you want to ... you learned so much,
you want to do something with that already. So in the beginning you are a
bit happy, that you finally go on an operation, you are excited and all, that's
the way it is in the beginning, a bit of fear, which is good fear, because in
that way you take care of yourself and you don't get into a routine and start
to take it easy [*lizrok hakhol*].

Doron, the paratrooper commander quoted before, had just received
a call-up for reserve duty in the Second Lebanon War (2006) when I
interviewed him. He compared the attitude of people around him at the
time of the interview and the feelings he and his comrades had during
Operation Defensive Shield in 2002. Some people were just waiting for
the action, for real combat.

It's like the people now [Second Lebanon War August 2006], there is activity, a war, and even in Lebanon, this is where we were drafted for, for this
we are here, it was more or less the same there, people were like, not just go
out to arrest a boy who knows a boy who knows a boy who threw a stone
on someone. We are there, inside, there are armed people ... [speaking about
Operation Defensive Shield in 2002].

Zadok, who served as a commander in the Nahal Brigade, recognized
these feelings of enthusiasm as well when there was a sudden call-up for
an operation that broke the routine of the soldiers:

At the moment there is a call up [*hakpatsa*] within half an hour everyone is
in their equipment ... within half an hour, everyone is excited, crazy. So yes,
that's the way it goes in the operation, then after the operation it stays like a
week or two, then you get back to the routine, till the next time that everyone jumps. It happens when there is a specific operation that is a bit different
than the routine, when there is an arrest you see all the platoon commanders
fight over who will get the operation. It breaks the routine of the guys, they
wait for it, this is what they are looking for.

Thus, routine is an important concept in the experience of soldiers in the
OPT. When it is broken, soldiers' morale is heightened and they seem to
be more motivated to perform their military duties. Later, we shall see
how the issue of routine contributes to the process of numbing soldiers
go through. Even though every arena has its own dynamics, and thus
its own routine, processes of numbing seem to set in everywhere. The
lack of interest in their work can also decrease the attention of soldiers
towards the civilians that cross the checkpoint and affect the way they
treat them.

Breaking the Routine: Operation Defensive Shield, a Case Study

Operation Defensive Shield (ODS) was an operation carried out by the IDF in the West Bank as a reaction to a series of suicide attacks within Israel, the last being the attack on the Park Hotel in the coastal city of Netanya on the eve of Passover in March 2002. At the beginning of April 2002, the IDF invaded all the large Palestinian cities except for Hebron and Jericho in order to uncover and destroy the infrastructure of Palestinian terrorist activity. For the period of the fighting, six large Palestinian cities were placed under curfew. The fighting in the refugee camp of Jenin became (in)famous due to the heavy combat and because of the subsequent visit of UN officials who were highly critical of the conduct of the Israeli military, stating that there had been an excessive use of violence. Besides the battle in Jenin, the siege of Yasser Arafat's compound was also one of the big events of the operation.

Many of the informants interviewed for this study served as conscript soldiers during this operation and it proved a formative experience for them. Here I would like to explore the routine of the work of Israeli soldiers from a somewhat different viewpoint. As noted before, sudden activities and unexpected operations break up the routine of soldiers. During Operation Defensive Shield, Israeli soldiers suddenly found themselves, in many instances for the first time, in actual situations of combat, of life-threatening danger and of exchanging fire with enemy troops. This operation, thus, threw soldiers out of their routine and into an extraordinary experience that stayed with them for a long time.

From the soldiers' stories, a sense of heightened motivation to participate in this military operation became clear. After the routine at the checkpoints, routine arrests and patrolling, suddenly there was a feeling of 'the real work', a sense of mission. The soldiers (finally) felt they were doing the work they were conscripted for; they were defending their state, defending their families. This contrast with the concepts I explored before is informative, as it gives us some insights into the way the Israeli soldier views his activities as a combat soldier: what he is doing and what he should be doing.

A few examples will be given here of soldiers participating in ODS and of the feelings that came with this experience. The naval captain quoted below, interviewed by Breaking the Silence, talks about his first combat experience on his boat during the operation and his impatience to commence shooting:

> I wanted to shoot, wanted to carry out the shooting from a boat that hadn't engaged in combat for a long time or killed a saboteur, and this represented a real opportunity. All of us [on the boat] felt very excited. Night after night boats returned from nightly duty without firing a single shot, and now we had such an opportunity. Our feeling was imbued by the aura of

'Defensive Shield', the [suicide] attacks preceding it and the tension. No wonder I wanted to shoot.

(BS fire opening)

Yossi had very vivid memories of ODS and most of the interview revolved around the stories of his experiences during the operation. He took part in the battle of Jenin as a young commander and lost comrades there. This experience of taking responsibility for his soldiers in real combat was immensely formative for him as a soldier, but also as a person in general. Coming from a leftist house in a *kibbutz*, he was determined to keep his head cool and not get carried away by a rage for revenge as many other soldiers did. He was very critical about the conduct of his fellow soldiers during this operation:[31]

> There were people, especially with the chain of bombings, it started with Hotel Park, I don't remember, there was this week of another 4–5 bombings, that's it, the IDF now has to take everything down. It's something that you felt. People said come on let's go in, we have to and all that, I didn't feel it, I got orders and I did it as good as possible, I didn't let myself ... I said okay there were bombings, the IDF has to respond, I'm in the IDF, I need to respond, without connection to whether it is legitimate or not. It would take away my self-respect if I thought 'he went and blew himself up so now I have to get in and kill everyone' and there were people who thought like that. To me it didn't happen. I ... really made the distinction, if you get into a house inside the refugee camp, after people were killed, and you do get into a house, treat with respect, and give water, and if there is a little girl help them. Isolate them but be in touch with them, and it could be that his brother is the one that is shooting at me from the front, but there is nothing you can do, you have to make this distinction, I did it, but not everyone made that distinction. There was horrible treatment [of Palestinians]. Really humiliating. In speech, in hitting, to get in there, boom, really like I need to pee, if there is no toilet, do it in the room, really nothing, erasing, like they are invisible, like there is no one there. No respectful treatment ...

What Yossi tells in this insightful story, is that he made a distinction between doing a job and possible emotions that were connected to the political situation. Making this division between professionalism and emotions is central in his discourse. Many other soldiers failed, in his eyes, and took revenge on the Palestinians for the death of Israelis by suicide bombers.

Haggai, who served in the Golani Brigade as a squad commander, remembers the attitude of the soldiers around him as well and also emphasizes the emotions that they experienced during ODS:

---

31. After the many suicide attacks by Palestinian terror organizations in Israel, many of the soldiers who participated in ODS felt they needed to take revenge, to avenge the Israeli victims of the attacks.

You have 18-year-old guys and you teach them to fight and you push them and they walk around with all those bullets and don't use them and suddenly they can. They teach him [the soldier] to shoot with all kinds of 'tools' he only saw in movies, and now he has the opportunity. And I also hate them [the Palestinians], as it happens I also hate them because I see them exploding on my friends every day on television. So why not ... of course there is a why not, but you don't think too much, you are 18–19 you are sure you are an adult.

The emotions that Yossi already mentioned before are eloquently put into words by Haggai; he tells about the excitement the soldiers felt when they finally could use materials they only knew from films, adding a playful element to their excitement for actions. He, furthermore, emphasizes their young age and the fact that within this situation young soldiers can easily blame the Palestinians for the situation they are in, for the deaths that occured in Israel at the time of the operation.

These factors can help us understand the processes soldiers go through within such operations, and the violence they are willing to use. While such operations are quite rare during the conscription of most soldiers, it is a complete different situation than the routine discussed earlier. The experience of most Israeli soldiers during big operations like Operation Defensive Shield could be seen as unusual 'breaks' within their otherwise monotonous and routine work. These experiences, stressful as they may be, seem to give soldiers an opportunity to live out their combat ideal. It furthermore strengthens the claim that the routine activities of Israeli soldiers in the OPT, of controlling another population, cause a degree of demoralization accompanied by attrition in the form of frustration, fatigue and the like, which in turn result in physical and mental numbing. This does not mean that while living this 'ideal' soldiers don't behave immorally, as we have seen in the quotes above. It, however, strengthens the claim of two different kinds of operations with different operational dynamics and a different effect on soldiers' behaviour.

Relations of Power

I was ashamed of myself the day I realized that I simply enjoy the feeling of power. I don't believe in it: I think this is not the way to do anything to anyone, surely not to someone who has done nothing to you, but you can't help but enjoy it. People do what you tell them. You know it's because you carry a weapon. Knowing that if you didn't have it, and if your fellow soldiers weren't beside you, they would jump on you, beat the shit out of you, and stab you to death – you begin to enjoy it. Not merely enjoy it, you need it. And then, when someone suddenly says 'No' to you, what do you mean no? Where do you draw the *chutzpah* from, to say no to me? Forget for a moment that I actually think that all those Jews are mad,[32] and I actually want peace and believe we should leave the Territories, how dare you say no to me? I am the Law! I am the Law here! And then you sort of begin to understand that it makes you feel good. I remember a very specific situation: I was at a checkpoint, a temporary one, a so-called strangulation checkpoint, it was a very small checkpoint, very intimate, four soldiers, no commanding officer, no protection worthy of the name, a true moonlighting job, blocking the entrance to a village. From one side a line of cars wanting to get out, and from the other side a line of cars wanting to pass, a huge line, and suddenly you have a mighty force at the tip of your fingers, as if playing a computer game. I stand there like this, pointing at someone, gesturing to you to do this or that, and you do this or that, the car starts, moves toward me, halts beside me. The next car follows, you signal, it stops. You start playing with them, like a computer game. You come here, you go there, like this. You barely move, you make them obey the tip of your finger. It's a mighty feeling. It's something you don't experience elsewhere. You know it's because you have a weapon, you know it's because you are a soldier, you know all this, but it's addictive. When I realized this ... I checked in with myself to see what had happened to me. That's it. And it was a big bubble that burst. I thought I was immune, that is, how can someone like me, a thinking, articulate, ethical, moral man – things I can attest to about myself without needing anyone else to validate for me. I thought of myself as such. Suddenly, I notice that I'm getting addicted to controlling people.

(BS Hebron)

This testimony, given by a former combatant to the organization Breaking the Silence, tells us about soldiers and the power that is bestowed upon them by the military, but also about how a soldier perceives this power and acts upon it. This soldier admits to the addictive features power has and he begins, contrary to all the expectations he has of himself, to enjoy the power he has over other people. He enjoys the ability to have people do whatever he wants them to do. And, when they do not comply, he gets angry because his power is questioned. He controls people and thrives in this situation. However, this is not the only form of power that exists within the context of the work Israeli soldiers perform in the OPT.

The actions and the dynamics of the work of Israeli soldiers relating to the Palestinian population can only be understood by examining the concept of power on multiple levels. The notion of power stands at the very core of the relationship between soldiers and Palestinians and of their function as soldiers in general. Different dimensions of the role power plays in the life and work of Israeli soldiers are the feeling of power soldiers have while performing their tasks, the actual power that is bestowed on them by the military and the perception of the power that they have. But power also comes in more subtle, implicit forms such as the power of a mere gaze, of bodily behaviour and even of dress.

---

32. Referring to the Jewish settlers in Hebron, who are known to be very rightist and hard-liners in their politics.

We can thus find a very direct form of power that is embodied in soldiers' behaviour, weapons and dress but also in the space within which they operate, especially the checkpoint. Its form and its sole purpose are very clearly embedded within unequal power relations. As I shall show shortly, the concrete form of power soldiers have over Palestinian civilians can lead to very dangerous and explosive situations.

Second, there is a high degree of structural power within an institution such as the military. The soldiers are under constant pressure to perform and to avoid punishment by their superiors. Foucault's concept of the disciplinary gaze is, then, very useful in this context, together with his ideas about the docile body. Soldiers' minds and bodies are disciplined within the military to think and act in a certain way by means of the structural elements incorporated in their socialization as soldiers.

This form of power is always present in the background of this research. However, often a more concrete form of power is being referred to. This power comes from the monopoly of violence the military has and its concrete dominance over the Palestinian civilian population.

Power and Responsibility

Young soldiers in the IDF are given a great amount of power. They control the Palestinian civilian population in the OPT and as the following quotes will show, this power is easily abused. Power for soldiers in the OPT springs from the responsibility that is given to them, especially at the checkpoints. Very young soldiers become checkpoint commanders, which means they are the ones to decide who can go through and who cannot, who has to be checked and who does not. With this responsibility, a strong feeling of power emerges. When a Palestinian, for example, does not listen to a soldier or starts an argument, this responsibility is questioned and the chances of such an encounter becoming violent (either verbally or physically) are relatively high. The feeling of dominance and power becomes so internalized that when it is questioned, a soldier can often react harshly.

Power and its addictive features numb the moral insights of soldiers. A person can get addicted to a sense of power and almightiness and can easily lose the ability to make morally just decisions. Guy, an officer who served with the paratroopers, talks about how he experienced the feeling of power:

> God, I can do everything. It's terrible, I told you I really, really tried for it not to happen, I was really … this power, and soldiers feel it. You can't use, it's possible to use it, yes when I get into an arrest operation let's say, in a house with someone, I have to show myself as powerful, I have to show this power with the weapon.

Liron realizes that the power of soldiers is related to the responsibility they are given. As he was a sniper, he gives the following example to illustrate this point:

> They give a lot of power to young officers. People of 22–23 get a lot of power. To the level of sitting with a sniper on the spot and telling him to shoot at everyone who is picking up a stone, they're telling the sniper who is a 19-year-old kid who is looking through the rifle sight and can also see a child of 10–12 years old. He has the option to shoot ...That power they're giving you is very blurred, very unclear.

The following quotes all point to the feeling of almightiness that soldiers get, the degree of power over other people and the way this power can be easily abused:

> There is a lot of tension, a lot of tension, they [the Palestinians] know that, however sad it is to say, they know that I'm in charge of their lives, that I decide who gets money and who doesn't get money, who ... gets to work and who doesn't. A lot of soldiers play with that, they like the power they have in their hands, the Arabs act very fake at the checkpoint, they know that you are sort of the king here, and it's very problematic.

> I'm just a kid. I was born yesterday. I derive my power from my uniform and my machine gun; it's what gives me the right to decide everything. And I do what I'm told to. That's the power I have and I use it. I can be the most enlightened and considerate person in the world but when I say: '*mamnu` tajawul, ruh `al beit*' [there's a curfew, go home] there is a period and four exclamation marks at the end of that sentence. It's non-negotiable. I don't care if I'm 18 or 17 or 21. I'm a soldier. I've got a gun and I'm from the IDF. I've got orders, and they better follow them.

> (BS Hebron)

The responsibility soldiers get during their work, their power to make decisions about the movement of people, about the way Palestinians should behave, comes with a great deal of concrete power for which many soldiers are not ready, either because of their age or because of their lack of experience with respect to the function they perform. In the quotes above one can sense a realization of the problematic side of having this power. However, this realization usually only surfaces after soldiers have finished their regular military service and after they have had some time to reflect on their activities as soldiers. While on duty, the feeling of controlling and having power over people seems to override emotions of empathy towards other persons or the global understanding by soldiers of what their activities really encompass.

Figure 12 Soldier having himself photographed in a Palestinian taxi (photo: courtesy of Breaking the Silence)

Disciplining Palestinians

'Discipline … is a type of power … comprising a whole set of instruments, techniques, procedures, levels of application, targets: it is a "physics" or an "anatomy" of power, a technology' (Foucault 1995: 215). As such, discipline is a very important 'technology' used by the military in order to establish its own power and authority. On a different level, it is used to express the power soldiers have and to re-establish it when it is questioned. Soldiers use mechanisms of discipline when they feel Palestinians need to be 'taught a lesson' because they do not listen, to make them see 'who is in charge'.

In line with Foucault's work, I would like to touch upon the subject of punishment and education by soldiers as a means of 'reinforcing or reorganizing their internal mechanism of power' (Foucault 1995: 215). As mentioned before, Israeli soldiers have a lot of responsibility and decision-making power at the checkpoint. When their power or authority is questioned, for example by a Palestinian who 'talks back' or refuses to do as he is told by the soldiers, one method employed is that of 'corrective punishment'. Against official military orders, but often with the knowledge of commanders in the field, soldiers, for example, can keep Palestinians waiting at the checkpoint for a few hours 'to dry up'.[33] Or they can take the keys of their cars and make them walk home for a few kilometres.

---

33. 'Dry up' or *yibush* is the detaining of Palestinians at a checkpoint for several hours, usually without any reason other than as 'punishment'.

Reasons given for such activities are 'to show who is in charge' and 'to teach them a lesson'; in other words to re-establish one's power through discipline. Palestinians, to use Foucault once more, are made docile.

Adam, the deputy company commander from the combat engineers, recalls the power that was given to the junior commanders under his own command:

> For example I find 15 people set aside at the checkpoint. But I know there were only seven names on the list. It's discipline by the Squad Commander. The Squad Commander is the king of the checkpoint ... It doesn't interest me if you stop explosives, it interests me that no one dares to try and take explosives. He makes other decisions. Sometimes it's an Arab that called him a name, the soldier, and I understand him 100 per cent ... but he will leave him two hours extra to 'teach him' [educate him] and that's the problem of the checkpoints. The simplest soldier is an educator.

This type of behaviour is also described in the next quote:

> It can be that other people would take the 2 people that were making problems, put them aside, blindfold them, put handcuffs, and put them in the sun, so they'll learn. No wonder there are people that do that ... Why? Because you haven't been home for 2 weeks, you do 8–8 at the checkpoint, you are hot, you are thirsty; it's the easiest.

Figure 13 Arrested boy detained (photo: courtesy of Breaking the Silence)

Within these quotes, the theme of 'educating' can be distinguished. From this discourse it becomes clear that an effort is made to establish one's power through methods that will teach the Palestinians something in such a way that they will not repeat their mistake. Ben-Ari et al. have rightly argued that similarities can be found between the way recruits are educated and disciplined in basic training and the way these recruits, in turn, use these mechanisms on the Palestinian civilians they face (Ben-Ari et al. 2004).

Distance and Proximity

Let me now turn to a third and final dynamic of the work arenas of Israeli soldiers in the OPT. In Chapter 2 I already discussed the issue of proximity and distance between perpetrator and victim and the effects that this can have on the perpetrator's actions. If we now take a look at the reality of the OPT, we can see how these concepts effect the practises of soldiers vis-a-vis Palestinian civilians.

Proximity and Distance at the Checkpoint

The effects of the checkpoints and its architectural organisation on the soldier who works within them are complex; different kinds of checkpoints have different effects on soldiers and because the same physical circumstances of a checkpoint can have different and even conflicting effects on different soldiers.

From observations it seems that the IDF has been making an effort to physically distance its soldiers from the Palestinians at the major checkpoints. In Lefebvre's words this is a conceived 'abstract' space where it seems there is no 'former history' and relationships are perceived as businesslike (Lefebvre 2007). Thick bulletproof glass ensures that the encounter between Palestinians and soldiers becomes a sterile meeting without eye contact, without direct communication through language and even without smell. The soldiers at the checkpoints are shielded off from the people they control and their sensory experience is diminished. These IDF measures are taken for security considerations, as soldiers are less likely to be attacked when standing behind glass.

The additional consequence of these security measures, however, is that the Palestinians around the soldiers become more abstract, impersonalized and are seen within a 'blurred view' (Grossman 1988) as a mass of 'Arabs' or 'Palestinians' or as categories such as 'the old man' or 'the pregnant woman' (Ben-Ari et al. 2004). Seen from a Palestinian perspective, a soldier becomes 'the bare face of the occupation and it becomes embodied in a person, a soldier who has immense power over your immediate destiny' (Hammami 2006: 24). They are reduced to 'the occupier'; the one with enormous power over the Palestinians.

The distance between soldiers and Palestinians can potentially make a soldier more indifferent to the person or 'category' he has in front of him. Following this view, also discussed by Grossman (1995), it seems that by distancing the soldiers physically from the Palestinian population the IDF makes it, perhaps unintentionally, easier for them to continue to carry out their work, controlling space and the people within it, in the Palestinian Territories.

This separation can, then, result in a greater degree of indifference towards 'the other'. The more distance between the soldiers and the Palestinians, the more their suffering or pleas become distant and the smaller the space will become that Palestinians inhabit in the moral universe of the soldiers.[34] Here, again, we should keep in mind the feelings of soldiers towards Palestinians, which are usually negative since Palestinians are seen as a hostile group or at least as an 'other'.

However, this is only one of the effects that distancing the soldiers from the passing Palestinians can have. Another effect can be that the distance of the soldiers from the sounds, the pleas and negotiations with the Palestinians (but also from the heat or the cold) can give them more space to behave in an empathetic way towards the people passing the checkpoint. This can happen because they are less likely to be influenced by factors such as the cold, the heat, frustration and fear, factors that, as we shall see shortly, can have a profound effect on the behaviour of soldiers. Both effects can happen simultaneously and depend, amongst other things, on the soldiers in question, the way they feel towards the Palestinians and on the exact circumstances of their specific work arena.

As stated before, most checkpoints are (still) open and the soldiers are in direct contact with the Palestinians. This proximity also has its own particular effects on soldiers' attitudes towards the latter. Just as the lack of sensory experiences (distance through glass, for example) can result in apathy, long hours at the checkpoint with hundreds of pleas and thus an overdose of sensory experiences can also cause indifference, as we shall see in the next chapter.

Distance during Arrests

During arrests, a different mechanism of separation comes into play. Whereas the distance at the checkpoint is managed through architectural measures, during arrests this method of distancing is not possible. The desired distance between soldiers and Palestinians, for security or other reasons, is more difficult to establish in these situations. During arrests,

---

34. A moral universe or a moral scope is an imagined space within which moral actors move and interact and as such is distinct from the above-mentioned 'moral region'. People who are considered to belong to the moral universe find themselves within the 'boundary in which moral values, rules, and consideration of fairness apply' (Opotow 1990: 1).

contact with the Palestinians in the house the soldiers enter is real and direct, and the dynamics of such situations are, therefore, profoundly different from those at the checkpoint.

In the conversations with soldiers, however, it becomes clear that it is important for them, and possibly for the military as a whole, to have as little contact with the Palestinian inhabitants as possible while in their houses. During arrests, these efforts are realized by avoiding confrontations and avoiding seeing the families of suspects or speaking to them in general. The operation should go as 'smoothly' as possible, which means, amongst other things, that no friction should arise between the soldiers and the inhabitants of the houses they enter.

Adam, a deputy company commander, is very much aware of the effect he, as a soldier within a private house, can have and emphasizes the efforts soldiers take to make an arrest go as smoothly as possible:

> A group of soldiers get into the house, and we try to do it as peaceful as possible. The best thing is if the man, when I knock on the door of the house, flees outside and the soldiers on the other side get him. Then he also shows himself and it goes smooth. And also his children, his mother I wouldn't have to face them. Usually you go into the house and frighten everybody with your gun, you don't frighten them God forbid with shooting or God forbid with pointing guns, but just by having the guns it's enough. You find him in the house, I will hold him until outside, then it's out of my hands, I won't God forbid question him, that is not my job and I don't, didn't know how to do that.

Adam makes very clear that he will do whatever he can in order not to confront the families living in the houses he enters. The perfect scenario he speaks of, when he doesn't even have to enter the house to get the suspect out again, shows the wish to engage as little as possible with the Palestinian residents. Nir, a commander in the Nahal Brigade, also emphasizes this effort when he talks about arrest missions he carried out as a squad commander:

> With arrests, you get info that is very 'fluid', it would happen at night, we would get a briefing about the house, where it is, etc., we would get a crew together, how exactly, how to walk there, do a scan of the house and all. We would be a securing force; we would get as little as possible in contact with the Palestinians, to do it as quiet as possible, not to break anything, so they won't accuse us later that we destroyed things. We would never touch, that's it. We take the guy out of the house, tie him up and call the Shabak,[35] check the ID, that's their work. We would search the house for weapons, and things you can find.

Great efforts are made to avoid communication with the Palestinians in order to avoid any kind of personal contact. Almost no conversations

---

35. General Security Service.

are conducted between soldiers and Palestinians, and certainly none on a personal level. This non-contact makes the work of soldiers easier. They slip into a strategy of denial (Cohen 2001) by looking away and not taking responsibility for the situation.

In the rare cases in which conversation does take place, the soldier sometimes engages in such conversations in a conscious effort to fight his own indifference. Golan is a person who, when conscripted within the IDF, had great trust in 'the system'; he was proud of his uniform and believed in the job he had to carry out. He served as an officer in the artillery corps. However, he became disillusioned with time by the misconduct and the disrespectful behaviour of his superiors. During his service he would make a conscious effort to make personal contact with the Palestinians he arrested: 'When I was sitting with the terrorist, it was very important for me to have some kind of contact, maybe from naivety, I was determined to stay a human being and not become a machine of hate and fear'.

However, Golan was an exception and his efforts were very personal. The discourse used here by Golan in which he emphasizes his own humanity and the importance of staying human himself, will be discussed later on when I will examine moral strategies used by soldiers.

The efforts made to have as little personal contact with the Palestinian 'other' as possible can, then, have several reasons. One of these is that speaking to the family members in a house being entered could cause extra friction and could possibly 'mess up' a smooth operation. On another level, this distance can serve as a guard against sympathizing with the 'other', who one is controlling. Such sympathy could lead to dilemmas that a soldier would prefer to avoid. Distancing is also used as a legitimating strategy; what one does not know (how the Palestinians really feel, what these operations do to them) one does not have to feel responsible for.

Proximity within 'Straw Widows'

Within 'straw widows' the contact with Palestinians is either more complicated, if the family that lives in the house stays put, or 'easier', when the family members are evicted altogether and the soldiers do not have to deal with them at all.

The following quote is from a commander who told Breaking the Silence about the difficulties he had when carrying out a 'straw widow'. He emphasizes that the closeness to the family in the house (to see them, to see and smell the food they were preparing, to see exactly how they were living) was too much for him to bear and made him distance himself from them. Carrying out his work as he was supposed to was, apparently, only possible for him by creating this distance.

That was one of the most difficult things I did, from a personal perspective, because when you are a commander you are always a bit lonely and suddenly you sit in a straw widow and one of the posts was to guard the family, I just couldn't look them in the eyes during the whole operation, it was very hard for me. They cook, you see what they eat, which is pitiful, you are confronted with all these things that you are not supposed to be confronted with. All the time the operation is nightly arrests, you are not confronted with the daily routine of the life of the family, you aren't confronted with the poverty. It was really difficult for me to sit in the room. I told some soldier I want you to be here, I can't be here anymore. I didn't explain to him why. I couldn't look them in the eyes, to see their looks or to see them sleep or not sleep, the fear.

(BS 45, translation EG)

In the following quote it again becomes clear that soldiers maintain a certain degree of distance. Nir talks about one of the 'straw widows' he occupied:

If you come and spend the night with a family, then you won't take them out of the house, we would be in the living room, they in the bedroom, someone is at the entrance guarding, so they don't have ... we are in the living room and there is no contact or passing. Whether they want it or not, it's not nice, true, there are people in your house, do whatever you want but you won't get into this area. They would know it; they knew soldiers would live with them. They can't do anything about it because we would be there anyway.

Nir clearly acknowledges the hardship experienced by the Palestinian inhabitants of the houses he occupies – 'it's not nice ... there are people in your house'. However, in his way of thinking, he does not have a choice but to do his job. This idea takes precedence over his discomfort with the situation concerning the family. The rationale and logic soldiers use to justify their actions will be discussed in the next part of this work.

Perceptions of Distance while on Patrol

Patrolling is one activity where the Israeli soldier does not necessarily engage in a lot of contact with the Palestinian population face to face. The presence of military vehicles on the roads around and within Palestinian villages and cities does, however, have an effect on the relationship between soldiers and Palestinian civilians.

Palestinians are likely to perceive soldiers patrolling with military vehicles as 'the army' or 'the soldiers' because they are barely visible as individuals. These men are merely shadows within heavily armed vehicles, vehicles which they do not get out of for security reasons. Many military vehicles incorporate security measures such as bars across the windows, further reducing the visibility of the people within them.

Just as the soldiers are reduced to mere figures within vehicles, the distance between them and the Palestinians also strengthens the depersonalization of the Palestinians in the eyes of the soldiers, a subject that has been discussed above. This distance can have the same effect as that discussed before in guarding the soldier against getting too involved. From a jeep it is easier to see a 'category' ('a young man' or 'an old farmer') than to see actual individual persons that you can relate to.

Figure 14 View from within a military vehicle, Hebron (photo: courtesy of Breaking the Silence)

Conclusion

In this chapter I have discussed a few important operational dynamics of soldiering in the Occupied Palestinian Territories, of which the importance became clear from the interviews held with Israeli soldiers. The routine they experienced during their work, the power that they were bestowed with and used and abused, sometimes even with pleasure. Finally the proximity and distance between soldier and Palestinian were discussed, as this issue, which relates to the use of space and taking control over space, is highly influential for soldiers' behaviour and decision making.

In the next chapter I will continue by discussing the different processes of numbing Israeli soldiers go through while working in the spaces described in Chapter 2. I will examine the influence, the properties and characteristics of these spaces and the work within them on their behaviour. I will discuss physical, emotional and cognitive processes of numbing, which, so I argue, influence soldiers' behaviour and use of violence considerably.

Chapter 5

Tired, Bored and Scared
Emotional, Physical and Cognitive Numbing

There's a very clear and powerful connection between how much time you serve in the Territories and how fucked in the head you get. If someone is in the Territories half a year, he's a beginner, they don't allow him into the interesting places, he does guard-duty, he's not the one to ... all he does is just grow more and more bitter, angry. The more shit he eats, from the Jews and the Arabs and the army and the state.

(BS Hebron)

The check posts are terrible, you curse everyone. It's a difficult experience, mentally, you don't see your home, you get pissed off, and you get orders from people that you wouldn't even talk to on the street.

As the soldiers quoted above make clear, there seems to exist a relationship between the spatial surroundings or work arena of a soldier, the operational dynamics present, such as the period of time he serves there and the routine he faces, and his 'mental state' or emotional state, as I will call it here. After a while of being subjected to these dynamics, the soldiers get 'bitter' and 'pissed off' as described above.

This state is a complex one and so are the processes that lead to it. I propose to analyze the processes Israeli soldiers go through during their work in the Occupied Palestinian Territories by looking at three different dimensions within soldiers' experience: the emotional, the physical and the cognitive. The emotional dimension consists of feeling 'bummed and burnt out', the physical dimension of being tired, cold and hot for example. Within the cognitive dimension we can see the blurring of categories around the soldier; he does not see the person in front of him as a clear individual 'I don't care if he's old, if he's a man, a woman ...'. All the categories used for identifying a person are blurred, a clear form of moral disengagement as defined by Bandura (1999).

I will put a focus on the sensorial experience of Israeli soldiers when working in the OPT and look at the way sight, smell, hearing and touch play a role in the way they perceive their surroundings and the way this influences their emotions and actions. Issues at hand are, for example, the noise, smell and dust of the checkpoints where soldiers stand for hours on end and the dirt, the heat and the cold and the sight of the suffering Palestinian population. Furthermore, work within the OPT, which usually takes place within an urban environment, involves impaired visibility and intense sounds (Ben-Ari 2008). All these issues involve the senses and point to their importance when trying to understand moral behaviour and decision making.

I argue that within these different dimensions, Israeli soldiers go through numbing processes that result in a more general state of numbing. This state of moral numbing, I will argue at a later stage, greatly influences the behaviour of soldiers and their moral decision making. Here I will discuss the implications and operational dynamics described in the previous chapters in all three dimensions, each dimension having its own different dynamic that leads to processes of moral numbing of the soldiers.

Anger, Boredom, Frustration and More: the Emotional Dimension

> Mentally, mentally, you're hot, August, ceramic vest, helmet on your head, and why? Because of them. Because of them [the Palestinians], and they stand in front of you ... and this goes through your mind.

Leavitt proposes to look at emotions as 'experiences that we recognize as involving both cultural meaning as bodily feeling. While they are subjectively felt and interpreted, it is socialized human beings – that is, thinking human bodies – who are feeling them in specific social contexts' (Leavitt 1996: 531). This is also how I will look at the emotions of soldiers in this work. These are socially constructed and shared between the soldiers. Emotions are recognized and expressed because of the meaning they have for a group or culture, a meaning that is shared by its members.

Emotions are an important part of the culture of human beings that anthropologists investigate. They have a distinct influence on the way people act within and react to the circumstances they find themselves in, just as these circumstances can be said to influence the emotions felt by people. Especially in this case, where the moral behaviour of soldiers is analyzed, emotions play an important role. Anger, frustration and all the other emotions that come into play during the work in the OPT at least partly guide the behaviour of soldiers.

Here the descriptions given by the soldiers themselves of the way they feel are used when speaking about emotions. In anthropological work on cultures different from the one of the researcher, it can be difficult to establish what is actually felt by a person, as the words he or she uses cannot be unambiguously translated into an emotion as the researcher knows it. In this case, where the informants speak the same language as the researcher,[36] some utterances about emotions and the way someone feels can, however, be used more or less directly.[37]

Within the interviews, Israeli soldiers usually divided the effects of the work at checkpoints into two categories: the physical hardships (*koshi phyzi*) and the mental or psychological hardships (*koshi mentali* or *nafshi*). Within this latter category (psychological hardship), emotions find their place. Emotions can vary from feeling angry, bitter, homesick, frustrated and unmotivated, to feelings of tension, loneliness or feeling worn out. All these emotions are part of a more general emotional state called attrition or *shkhika*. Here, I will discuss this state and the particular emotions of soldiers it contains within the different arenas of work described earlier.

Shkhika sums up the negative influence of the work soldiers perform on their emotional or physical state. Such influences vary from space to space and include weather conditions, lack of sleep and the monotony of the work. These factors can lead to emotions of frustration, boredom and irritation, for example. These can all be grouped under the label 'emotional attrition' and they can be of great influence on the way soldiers behave and make their (moral) decisions in the field. Dar, Kimhi, Stadler and Epstein show how this is not unique to the Al-Aqsa Intifada, but was already observable in the First Intifada (Dar et al. 2000: 299). Not all emotions will be discussed here, however, only the ones that are clearly shared by the soldiers while they serve within specific arenas within the OPT.

Emotional Attrition at the Checkpoint

The concept of attrition is very central in the discourse of soldiers. When asking soldiers about how they felt when standing at a checkpoint or during guard duty, for example, most if not all answers included the word '*shkhika*' or '*shokhek*'.[38] Yoel, a former commander from the tank division, emphasizes the effects attrition can have on a soldier; effects strong enough to make a soldier 'go crazy':

> It's the *shkhika*, the *shkhika*, the *shkhika* during the operational period of the service [*kav*], about 4 months, you do 8–8–8–8 or four–four or 12–12 or 6–6,[39] and sometimes because some mistakes we have eight–two, guard

---

36. This does not mean that the researcher understood the language of the informants at all times, especially when slang or professional jargon was used.
37. Of course, for this text a translation from Hebrew into English is necessary.
38. In Hebrew the word attrition (*shkhika*) can also be used as a verb.
39. Yoel is referring to hours of duty and hours of rest respectively (for example eight hours guard duty, eight hours off duty and then eight hours of guard duty again).

eight hours, get down for two, guard for eight hours again. During twenty-four hours. It happens. In those four months you acquire a huge repertoire of songs, that you learn to sing, you develop hobbies that you never thought were possible, and there are people that in order to deal with it shoot, or something, and there are people that go crazy. Not after four months, but after a year, a year and a half.

The emotions that Yoel mentions are those of boredom because of the hard routine of the guard shifts and a feeling of frustration that can even result in violent outbursts by a soldier, such as the shooting for no apparent reason and 'going crazy'. Eviatar mentioned how attrition caused by work at the checkpoint could make soldiers act in irrational ways. Sometimes they start to see suspects where there are none: 'For the first 2 weeks it's ok, you stick to the rules, but after a while, you guard 8 hours every day, you don't sleep enough, you are tired, you are worn out, the situation finishes you, physically and mentally and then comes the suspicion, people react in a non-rational way'.

A former soldier from the Givati Brigade, Offir, who served at many checkpoints, emphasizes the difficulties of the long hours and the routine, characteristics that are, as we have seen, typical of work at the checkpoint. He, furthermore, asserts how commonly shared those emotions were during his service: 'The difficulties for the soldier were the mental problems in his head, to cope with the days, the hours, the routine. That was what the soldier went through. Everyone went through it, at least those that were with me'.

Other features of the work at the checkpoints that contribute to the processes of emotional attrition, apart from the routine and the long hours mentioned before, are the continuous line of people making pleas, the discussions and negotiations about the right to pass through the checkpoint and dealing with daring youngsters.[40]

As the soldiers control the passage through the checkpoint, people come to them continuously with pleas to let them through, with explanations about visits to the hospital or the doctor's or about needing to get to work. This is especially confronting when the soldiers are not behind glass but standing in direct contact with the Palestinians who are passing through the checkpoint. Proximity to the passing Palestinians is a dynamic, as mentioned earlier, that influences the behaviour of soldiers. The Palestinians want to go through to continue their daily business and the soldier on duty has to decide whether or not to let them do so, based on his own deliberation and on the rules set by his commanders. Sometimes he will listen to the reasons given by passers-by, sometimes he will check a permit or ID card and sometimes he will refuse to listen altogether. This behaviour is often arbitrary. The continuous

---

40. These youngsters are also known as '*shabab*'; young men that hang around waiting for some action, fun and/or trouble.

pleading often frustrates the soldiers and makes them angry. The 'wearing down' of soldiers is at times even used as a conscious strategy by the Palestinians to get through a checkpoint after being denied passage: '[Y]ou have to simply wear them [the soldiers] down by not giving up' (Hammami 2006: 25).

In footage taken by the IDF at the Hawara Checkpoint[41] on the outskirts of Nablus in 2004, Israeli soldiers negotiating with Palestinians can be seen getting more and more aggressive, both verbally and physically. In the explanations given by the soldiers for their behaviour, it becomes clear that they act out of frustration and anger and from a desire 'to teach them' (the Palestinians) how one should behave at the checkpoint and who is in charge. However, boredom and frustration are not the only emotions experienced by soldiers at checkpoints or during guard duty; soldiers sometimes emphasized their feeling of insecurity and fear. Work at checkpoints that were open and where the soldiers stood in direct contact with the passing Palestinians was especially accompanied by feelings of tension and of being 'sitting ducks':

I didn't like these checkpoints, but ... (Q: 'Why?') Also its boring, also you are like a duck in a shooting range, if I was a terrorist with some experience, there would be no soldier that would survive the checkpoint, it would be enough to look at a checkpoint for a month, to know exactly how many soldiers, where they stand, you see it, everyone knows it, they are less alert, [they want] to pass the time ... When you do a checkpoint nonstop for half a year, it's wearing out, it finishes people, a terrorist that tries to hit a checkpoint usually succeeds, usually.

However, as this soldier says, this tension or alertness dwindles as time goes by and as soldiers spend more and more time at the same checkpoint, doing the same work. They become less alert, less afraid and increasingly bored, making them a perfect target for an attack.

Tension and Fear: Emotions during Arrests and 'Straw Widows'

Most of the emotions of fear and tension were reserved for operations such as arrests and the occupation of 'straw widows'. Risks here are higher due to the inherent uncertainties of the situation. In these spaces the emotions that came with uncertainty and insecurity were plentiful, as the following quotes show: 'It was the first time I made a [straw] widow by myself as a commander of a force. That's a very scary thing, especially when you're in Balata, which is one of the more hostile refugee camps there is, it was a house with a lot of families' (BS 45, translation EG).

---

41. As this film did not show what the IDF envisioned it did not come out, until a soldier decided to leak it.

Talking about his first experiences in the OPT, this former soldier from an elite unit of the paratroopers says:

> In the beginning it's scary, there were a few bombings in Jerusalem last year, they put us inside Bethlehem in neighbourhoods that are known to be enemies, when you go in you know that for sure there will be shooting, for sure there will be incidents ... So there I remember we got in and it was really very scary. In the end there was nothing, we did the arrest as we should have done and all, but when we got out of the cars and ran to the house, then my heart was really pounding, you look everywhere, you are ready, it was really scary.

As these examples show, we cannot lose sight of the fact that some of the work Israeli soldiers perform within the OPT is dangerous and carries risks to their safety. As the quote in the beginning of this chapter made clear, soldiers who find themselves in a state of restlessness can also experience a high degree of tension. This state is reached when tension is always present. Danger can be anywhere and can come from any side. Danger comes from the enemy but there is also pressure to perform well in front of the commanders and pressure from the home front, both of these also playing an important role: 'It's wearing you out, because you almost don't have time to rest, in your time of rest you also work, all the tensions you have around you, from the settlers, from the commanders, tensions from home, you are under tremendous tensions from all directions all the time'.

Interestingly, while some soldiers did relate their feelings of fear, many others said that to their own surprise they did not feel any, even if, looking back at past experiences, they could not imagine not feeling afraid back then. It seems that at the moment of action, fear is not much of an issue for soldiers who have been socialized not to feel or even think about it. Yariv, who had just been released from the elite section of the Nahal Brigade a few months before our interview, remembers:

> Most of the operations are routine, they're routine already. The first operation I was in was in Jenin and then the adrenaline flowed. (Q: 'Was it fear or adrenaline?') Adrenaline, not fear, you don't even think about fear. I don't know. There was a month and a half full of operations, six operations where wanted men were killed or wounded within a month and a half. And then our team commander asked us if we were afraid ... we don't think about fear, every time, if the operation is of size you have a pre-briefing of about two–three days, you just have more adrenaline, not more fear. Not fear. I don't know.

Offir puts into words how being part of a 'bigger whole' or system, like the military, can make you feel strong and fearless:

> The IDF makes you not be afraid of anything, you can do everything, everything is in your head, the fear is psychological. (Q: 'So there wasn't any

fear?') What do you call fear? (Q: 'For example at night or the feeling that you might get hurt.') When you're inside the system you are not conscious of what you do, you have confidence in what you do, you are a body ... and you are serious on everything, you don't think twice. You are very decisive, concentrated, if you don't have it then it's better that you're not there.

Thus, emotions of real fear are not particularly acute in the experience of soldiers. Being part of a system such as the military empowers the soldiers and does not give feelings of fear any room to surface. While in action and carrying out their mission emotions of fear seem to be repressed, as we were able to see in the above quote about Operation Defensive Shield where 'adrenaline flowed'[42] but where no fear was felt. Tension, however, is present in any uncertain situation soldiers find themselves in.

Emotions and their Effects

All emotions discussed above, such as boredom, frustration, anger, fear and feelings of tension, can be called numbing emotions as they have a numbing effect on the moral professionalism of soldiers. Soldiers feel frustrated, they are worn down and they easily act this out on the Palestinians passing through the checkpoint or whom they meet on the streets during patrols. Even emotions that are apparently not numbing, such as fear and tension, can also have a numbing effect on one's moral effectiveness. The moral behaviour of soldiers will be discussed in the next chapter; here it is enough to emphasize the relationship between emotions that arise from the nature of the work Israeli soldiers perform within the OPT and their subsequent behaviour.

Because soldiers are bored, frustrated, tense or afraid, their behaviour is less deliberated and can, thus, be harsh or humiliating towards the Palestinians they are confronted with. This behaviour can be verbal but it can also become physical as testimonies and reports of human rights organizations show. A twenty-four-year-old Palestinian man, who was detained at a checkpoint and abused by soldiers, reported the following:

After that, the two soldiers grabbed me by the shoulders and dragged me to the checkpoint, about thirty meters. While they dragged me, they hit and kicked me. At the checkpoint they bound my hands very tightly with plastic handcuffs. I heard the first soldier shout in Hebrew but didn't understand what he was saying. Another guy who was being held there told me, 'Lie down on the ground'. While he was talking to me, the first soldier hit me in the legs, and I fell on my face. Another guy tried to wipe the blood from my lips, but the soldier shouted at him. He mumbled that he was sorry he couldn't do something to help. Ten minutes later, the two soldiers picked me

---

42. Adrenaline can signify that a person is afraid; in this interview, however, I understood it to mean excitement.

up by the shoulders and threw me into a concrete cell, about two meters long and one meter wide and then left.[43]

This testimony gives us an example of the sometimes harsh behaviour of Israeli soldiers. From the statement of this Palestinian, the frustration and anger of the soldier involved becomes clear: even though he has been restrained, the Palestinian man is still hit and shouted at, in clear violation of international and Israeli military ethics.

Hot, Cold and Tired: the Physical Dimension

It's difficult, it's not easy and not ... it's hot and cold and in all weather you are there.

Attrition can also be expressed in physical terms. Physical characteristics of the work that soldiers perform and the places they perform it in, influence the way they feel, both emotionally and physically, and therefore influence their actual behaviour. Winslow already mentioned in her study on the Canadian airborne in Somalia how 'environmental stressors have an impact on soldiers' health ... and [that] climate can affect group cohesion and attitudes toward out groups' (Winslow 1997: 225). Especially the monotone landscapes soldiers serve in, and also the lack of comfort compared to what they are used to back home and their inability to escape the physical environment, influence the group (ibid.).

Another physical aspect of the work of soldiers is that of their own bodies and dress and the embodiment of their emotions. The bodies of soldiers, as Foucault (1995) has noted, are made docile by the military and for this reason discussing the way bodies play a role within power relations and communication, for example, is important in understanding the experiences of soldiers.

The body, it has been recognized, is part of human social culture, influences it and is in turn influenced by it. The body and the modifications made to its surface (like clothing, adornment and makeup) make the social order within which we live clear. The surface of the body, furthermore, consists of 'signs of the cultural boundary between the self or person and its social and natural object world' (Turner 1995: 146).

The importance of seeing the body and its modifications as significant becomes very clear in the military case where stars, stripes and other decorations on the uniform represent who you are and where you fit within the military hierarchy. As Winslow wrote: 'In some parts of the world men scar cheeks to show their place in society. In the army they scar their shoulders in order to show their rank and they mark their

---

43. This testimony was collected by the Israeli human rights organization, B'tselem, www.btselem.org as accessed on 24 May 2007.

chests with the history of their accomplishments' (Winslow 2003: 26). The uniform also emphasizes the difference between soldiers and civilians; it creates a boundary between different groups of people.

Body language is also of importance; the posturing of soldiers, the way soldiers stand, the way they show their guns, the way they gesture while at the checkpoint or within a Palestinian house, the way Palestinians stand in line, lower their eyes or fiercely look the soldiers in the eye. These are all issues concerning the body and of importance when trying to understand the way soldiers feel and behave.

Importantly, this issue is closely related to power; to one dominant and one subordinate party facing one another. The senses and the layers that cover the body signify boundaries, otherness, difference and dominance. The military body is a very masculine one, for example, and it can be argued the Palestinian body, in its subordinate state, is feminized within the military context of the OPT (see Amireh 2003).

In her work on the misconduct of Canadian soldiers in Somalia, Razack shows how the soldiers emphasized the cruelty of the circumstances they found themselves in: the heat, the dust and the Somali youths who irritated them and drove them to the limits of their patience (Razack 2000). The experiences of the Canadian soldiers Razack talks about are in many ways comparable to the situation of Israeli soldiers at the checkpoints; the soldiers have to face all weather, dust, mud and, as mentioned before, the continuous pleas of passing Palestinians. Hammami writes about how this is viewed from the Palestinian point of view: 'We know when the soldiers look at us in line, what they see are pushy, uncivilized animals who create chaos, and lie – yes, this is the physical reality they have created by their presence' (Hammami 2006: 26).

I will focus here on aspects connected to what Israeli soldiers call 'physical hardship' in relation to their work in the OPT. Furthermore, communication and body language will be discussed as both issues are related to the physical aspects of work in the OPT.

Physical Attrition at the Checkpoint

The soldiers at checkpoints are often exposed to harsh weather conditions such as wind, rain, snow and scorching sun in summer. The open checkpoints, in particular, are difficult working arenas from this point of view. Not much scholarly work has been done on the effects of heat and cold on the performance of soldiers, but from the stories of soldiers who have served during various conflicts and wars it becomes clear that they are influential. Kobrick and Johnson (1991), for example, mention S.L.A. Marshall's work (1947) in which he observed 'men ceasing to function in both extreme heat and deep cold, although they were physically unharmed' (Kobrick and Johnson 1991: 223).

From the material collected for this study, it became clear that weather conditions and other physical elements of their work influenced the degree of physical attrition experienced by soldiers. A soldier from a paratrooper unit relates his experiences in the cold region of the Southern Hebron Hills where he was posted for four months. He mentions the cold, being worn out and this resulting the then abuse of power by the soldiers:

> In that period we would do 10 hours of back up duty on the patrol routes and then we would go up for guard-duty, and then we would do shifts in the headquarters. We would 'grind' our asses off there. And all this in the winter. You probably know what the winter is like in the Southern Hebron Hills, it's snow and it's a crazy wind and it's cold and we would be pitiful … we got winter overalls [*hermoniot*] and Canadian shoes, but the platoon commander said that Canadian shoes and winter overalls weren't operational because it makes you cumbersome and you can't move … its horribly cold, and from all this 'grinding' [*thkina*] and boredom, yes you are cold, so you stop a truck that comes through the checkpoint and tell them: now you stop here, you are the shield against the wind, because the truck blocks the wind, and now you stop here and be my wind shield. Like that we hid behind him for like half an hour – okay you can go now, yalla, go. And that was it, those were the checkpoints.

> (BS 36, translation EG)

Furthermore, as we have seen in several of the previous quotations, fatigue is a very important physical condition that strongly influences soldiers' behaviour. A severe lack of sleep is what almost every soldier complains about and mentions when speaking about his military service. Williams shows in one of the few sociological studies on sleep how it 'is intimately bound up with emotion, trust and ontological (in)security' (2007: 153).

A popular Israeli saying, usually used when referring to reservist duty, is that once a man dons a uniform he immediately becomes hungry, horny and tired. Military service is, then, closely associated with bodily functions and needs. The above saying points to the need for food, sleep and sexual relations. The body of a soldier is thus very central to his soldiering experience. As a former soldier quoted before said: '[Y]ou're always tired, you're always hungry, you always have to go to the bathroom'.

Communication

Communication can be conducted on several levels. It can be verbal, but most communication is, in fact, established through eye contact or gesturing, making the body a very central part of it. Contact between two strangers usually begins with a look and is then followed by speech.

That is, if both parties speak the same language. Verbal communication between Israeli soldiers and the Palestinians is often very problematic; most soldiers do not speak Arabic and most Palestinians, except for those who have worked in Israel or who have spent time in Israeli prisons, do not speak Hebrew. Miscommunication can lead to misunderstandings, for example when a soldier tells a person to stop and the person does not understand what he is saying and thus carries on. This, in turn, can lead to a reaction on the part of the soldier that can eventually lead to violence by the soldier, verbal or physical, directed against the Palestinian. The following examples show how (mis)communication can play a role in the relationship between soldiers and Palestinians:

> I would tell my soldiers 90% of the world's conflict is from a lack of understanding, 90% of this lack of understanding is because of lack of communication and 90% of communication is through speaking. So if you cannot speak with the population, you start from a point that is not equal. The joke in the army is 'why do I need to speak Arabic, I have my gun'. In our company someone made a dictionary of spoken Arabic with all kinds of sentences, we copied and distributed it in the section. It didn't help much, but a little.

> The point in what I'm saying now is there specifically was a miscommunication between us and them. Many times they had a permit, but you would take him, treat him as a suspect, bind him, you blindfold him, while all he did was go to work and you hold him with you at the checkpoint for hours.

> (BS 45, translation EG)

To this we can add the fact that soldiers minimize their communication with Palestinians as much as they can, as we have seen before. At checkpoints such as Qalandia and many other places, like DCOs,[44] for example, the communication between Israeli soldiers and Palestinians is indirect (through megaphones or intercoms), making it almost exclusively one-sided in the form of orders and short sentences. The soldiers are not physically present, being hidden from the public by walls or dark glass.

Zanger states that the proceedings at the checkpoint can be seen as speech acts that follow a predetermined protocol incorporating utterances such as 'ID', 'permit', 'Where are you going?' and 'Where did you come from?' (Zanger 2005). These short sentences, usually ending in a question mark, are uttered again and again, hour after hour, day after day, without ever developing into full conversations.

Communication or the lack of it is also a way for soldiers to 'other' the Palestinians in order to emphasize their otherness and the distance between 'them' and 'us'. When the communication between parties is

---

44. District Coordination Office of the IDF, where all permits are issued for the Palestinian population of the OPT.

Figure 15 Palestinian arrestee in military vehicle (photo: courtesy of Breaking the Silence)

short and impersonal, or even non-existent, 'otherness' is enhanced and reinforced.

Body Language

> [They seemed bigger] not only because of their age but mainly because of the many gadgets that swelled them up and bulked up their bodies, bodies that, when their owners are in their other world, the private one, the intimate one, are maybe even skinny.[45]

Mauss extensively studied bodily techniques and the way they were passed on from generation to generation (1979). Such bodily techniques include ways of swimming and working but also ways of giving birth or expressing dominance over others. The way our body performs certain actions is culturally ingrained in us, Mauss asserts.

Foucault has done influential work on the body as well, especially on the control of the body through the internalization of rules and habits (1995). Both Mauss' and Foucault's work make us realize the importance of looking at bodily behaviour and its meanings. As Foucault has specifically shown in his work, this is especially true concerning soldiers and their 'docile bodies'. These bodies, I argue, can, in their turn, also keep power structures intact.

The uniforms they wear and the weapons they carry materialize the power that soldiers have. Their body with its 'adornments' is a central tool in emphasizing this power; it makes clear who they are, how strong they are and it also makes a clear distinction between them and the Palestinian civilian population around them.

Because of the uniforms soldiers wear, often only their faces and hands are visible for the other. This also has its effect on the communication between both parties. Most important is the inequality between the two; on one hand, the dominant soldier in uniform, on the other, the Palestinian civilian who is in the role of the submissive, the one who has no choice but to do as the soldier says.

Not only the uniforms and the weapons are important in this sense, body language is also a tool used by soldiers to emphasize their power. Accompanying the speech acts mentioned before are gestures that tell people to 'come forward' or 'stay back' or 'go home'. Even though the means of communication are few, the power of the soldiers is established by them at all times.

Posture has always been important in any combat situation conducted face to face (see Grossman 1995). In the same way that Dutch soldiers

---

45. From a letter to a soldier in Hebron by an activist from MachsomWatch. The letter was translated from Hebrew by George Malent and published in the *Occupation Magazine*, see www.kibush.co.il/show_file.asp?num=26608 as accessed on 11 July 2008.

in peace-keeping operations take off their helmets to communicate more easily with the civilian population in places like Iraq or Afghanistan and to show that they are not aggressive (see van Baarda and Verweij 2006: 4–6), Israeli soldiers at checkpoints will hold their guns high, wear sunglasses and stand strong to show the Palestinian civilian population who is in control. The dark reflective sunglasses often worn by Israeli soldiers contribute to the distance between soldier and Palestinian, as one cannot make eye contact through the dark glass (Ben-Ari et al. 2004).

It seems, then, that the senses are blocked as much as possible so as to not see, hear, smell or touch the 'other'. The less soldiers use their senses in the course of their contact with the 'other' the easier it becomes for them to carry out their work of controlling another people in the practice of occupation.

The way soldiers feel physically – tired, cold, hot or dirty – has a profound effect on their emotions, which were discussed above. Soldiers' emotions, especially anger and frustration, can be heightened by the level of their physical (dis)comfort as many soldiers interviewed indicated. Furthermore, the way they communicate and use their body to send out messages or to distance themselves from the Palestinians shows the importance of the physical dimension and its implications for the work of Israeli soldiers within the OPT.

Unclear Categories and Uncertainty: the Cognitive Dimension

The way one sees and understands one's surroundings and the way one categorizes them belong to the cognitive dimension of soldiers' experience. Here, this principally entails the way Israeli soldiers distinguish between friend and foe and the way they categorize the people they deal with and the work they carry out.

Friend or Foe

> I think your judgment gets a little impaired when every day … when your enemy is an Arab or somebody else who in your eyes … like, you don't look at him as a person standing in front of you, but as the enemy, and this is the word for him: enemy. He is not a dog, he is not some animal, you don't think of him as inferior, he simply doesn't count. Period. He is not … he is your enemy, and if he's the enemy, you kill him. And if it's him that you kill, once you've killed him, then it seems that there's nothing worse you can do to him, but apparently there is.
>
> (BS Hebron)

In the quote above the process of depersonalization becomes obvious. The Palestinian is not dehumanized, but made into an entity or category.

As such, he or she is not seen as an individual person anymore; he or she becomes 'the enemy' (see Ben-Ari et al. 2004).

The distinction between an innocent civilian and the violent enemy is a very problematic one in the OPT and in other asymmetrical conflicts. The fact that you do not know who your enemy is heightens the tension of soldiers along with their feeling of insecurity. They can never know if and from where they will be attacked. One soldier described this feeling as a 'negative high', a constant sensation of restlessness. The examples below from interviews with a squad commander and a soldier make this point clear:

> To recognize who is an enemy and who is a friend? You can't really say until something happens ... an operation ... it happened often that we would go out in the day time in a village, which is the most scary that can be, from every side there can be a terrorist, they can shoot, there you really can't say who is who, you just have to open your eyes all the time, be ready, it's much more scary and more dangerous.

> At a checkpoint there is the danger of explosives. With all the humanity ... if explosives pass [through] then ... that's the ambivalence at the checkpoint. You can call it ambivalence. The two-sidedness you can call it. On one side most are innocent ... on the other side in that population there consists of people that are abusing this; I'm not saying this in a political way but as a soldier.

When the distinction between an innocent passer-by and a possible terrorist is unclear for a soldier, one mechanism to deal with this is to treat everyone as a potential attacker and thus as the enemy. Seeing a whole population as hostile can easily lead to the harsh treatment of innocent people and to unnecessary violence against them. This can be seen as what Miller and Moskos (1995) have called the 'warrior strategy' that soldiers adopt in order to deal with their unclear position vis-a-vis the 'other'. This reaction, in part, also arises from feelings of fear and stress. Processes of 'othering' or making another person into a negative 'other' are, then, triggered by feelings of insecurity caused by the difficulty of distinguishing between friend and foe.

Dirty Work at the Checkpoint: Unclear Categories

As already discussed before, policing work in general, and especially the work at the checkpoints, is basically seen by soldiers as the most dirty work one can do during service within the OPT. In Hebrew it is called *avoda shehkora* or, literally, 'black work'. The work is first of all seen as unsophisticated and, therefore, far from the ideal activity of a combat soldier. Elite combat units usually do not participate in work at checkpoints. As discussed earlier, what many soldiers are looking for is 'action', anything that will get them out of their routine. The work at the checkpoint is, then, seen as doing precisely the opposite and is, as such, viewed as inferior. Furthermore, this type of work is seen as very difficult work because of its monotonous and boring character, but also because of the uncertainty it entails and the unclear situations soldiers find themselves in throughout their time at a checkpoint.

Dror, a platoon commander who had many soldiers under his command who worked at checkpoints, emphasizes this issue:

> Bottom line [*tahles*] [work at the checkpoints], it is the 'dirty work', there isn't much dynamics. You get a certain work habit, everyone his own. It depends on the dynamics of the people you work with at the checkpoint. There isn't a lot of curiosity. Actually you have seen it all after your first checkpoint … there is no dynamics or excitement. If you find something you're happy because it doesn't happen a lot, it's a matter of luck, of the situation.

Adam, however, emphasizes another aspect of the work at the checkpoints: the uncertainty that is felt by soldiers during their work. As a deputy company commander who spent many hours visiting the checkpoints where his soldiers were stationed, he faced many instances where situations were not clear-cut and where he had to make decisions on the spot:

> I just want to know that no one enters Nablus that doesn't have anything to do there. The IDF wanted to separate the villages from the cities. So if there is someone from a village, he doesn't have any reason to go to Nablus. They had doctor's permits, but we would know exactly where the doctors were and if there was a doctor in their village or the one next to it. The situation is very hard, there aren't clear-cut answers, there aren't clear-cut orders.

Adam emphasizes here that 'there aren't clear-cut answers' and there are no 'clear-cut orders', and this creates a situation of not knowing or confusion that is felt to be problematic by the soldiers. If there are no clear-cut orders, you have to make decisions on your own. While commanders are used to doing this, for soldiers it is more difficult and can produce dilemmas as the last example (where people want to cross the checkpoint to go to a doctor, while the orders are to keep people who do not live there from going into Nablus) shows.

Conclusion

In this chapter I discussed the implications of the spaces soldiers work within on three different dimensions of their daily experience; the emotional, the physical and the cognitive. I have tried to show how processes of numbing within different dimensions are triggered by the effects of heat, cold, uncertainty, tension and fear and how these can affect the behaviour and actions of soldiers.

Within the emotional dimension, soldiers related feelings of boredom, frustration, anger, tension and fear. Within the physical dimension, weather conditions and a lack of sleep, for example, were recognized as influential for the behaviour of soldiers. Furthermore, their bodies and their body language were shown as being important in their relations to and communication with Palestinians in the setting of the OPT. Finally, within the cognitive dimension, the blurred categories of 'friends and foes', the difficulties of distinguishing between them and the effect of this on the work at the checkpoint were discussed. All these issues not only influence the behaviour of soldiers in general by numbing them emotionally and physically, but can also lead to the numbing of the moral ability or moral competence of Israeli soldiers. I argue that these conditions do, indeed, lead to a general state of moral numbing. In the next chapter this numbing will be discussed in further detail.

CHAPTER 6

BLURRING MORALS
the Numbed Moral Competence of Soldiers

Having looked at the spaces Israeli soldiers move and work within and the implications of the operational dynamics of these spaces on their behaviour, I will now discuss the issue of numbing within what could be categorized as a fourth dimension: the moral one. This moral numbing, I argue, can be seen as the end product of the different processes of numbing discussed above. I define moral numbing as the numbing of the ability to recognize and act upon a moral aspect of a specific situation. The ability to do this also has been called moral professionalism (Verweij 2007). After introducing this concept in order to understand the issue of moral numbing better, I will discuss two central issues relating to moral numbing: cognitive blurring and detachment.

Moral Professionalism

> The thing that I managed to understand only later, honestly because that place makes you emotionally detached and you aren't really able to figure out what goes on there ... I understood how inhumane it was. How evil it is to do this to people. To take them and stick them on top of each other; to make them stand like this for twenty minutes, and not because of some security necessity, but because the soldiers acted out of inertia and found an interesting way to pass their guard duty.
>
> (BS Hebron)

An acknowledgement rings out in this quote as this soldier conveys how he only came to understand later on what he and his comrades did when they were serving in the military. This shows the detachment of the soldiers from acknowledging what is right and wrong or from knowing how human beings should be treated. An important notion here is moral professionalism, which can be defined as being morally competent or as recognizing the moral dimension of a situation and being able to make the morally responsible decisions at the right time (Verweij 2007). In the example above, this professionalism was clearly not present.

Professionalism, on a moral level, means doing one's job according to values and norms that come from one's society, one's upbringing and one's professional training. Militaries try to ensure that their soldiers are morally professional so that they will know how to act in a morally responsible way in each situation that they encounter. For this purpose, militaries make an effort to train their soldiers accordingly. Richardson et al. (2004) have used the term 'moral fitness' to emphasize this learnable aspect of moral awareness.

What happens, however, when the circumstances are not ideal or clear-cut? When numerous factors influence the behaviour of soldiers in ways they could hardly have been trained for? The work of Israeli soldiers is, indeed, work that is often unpredictable and many morally unclear factors are involved, especially when dealing with civilians. Together with all the implications discussed earlier, Israeli soldiers often find themselves in morally ambiguous situations. Here I will go into some of the moral implications of the work arenas described in Chapter 3 for Israeli soldiers. We could, then, call these moral implications and the numbing of the moral competency of soldiers the end result of the emotional, physical and cognitive processes.

> You just become like a robot, I don't know how to explain it. There's a stage where ... either routine or fatigue when you no longer have the strength to be patient, you have no strength to ... Someone comes and throws a remark which he shouldn't, like 'What do you want from me?' which is legitimate in his opinion, and even in my opinion, that person lives there, you know ... It's a street where they're allowed to pass, and a soldier comes and stops him and checks him and searches him and his kids are there and his family is there, and its [sic] humiliating for him, and there's a stage when you just don't care anymore, old man, not old man, you check them all.
>
> (BS Hebron)

At the time, the soldier in the above example did not recognize the moral dimension of the situation he was in. He explains this in terms of routine and fatigue. He did not care anymore and just did his work without considering the context in which the situation took place, of who he was checking and of why he was checking this person.

Eviatar, who chose a professional career in the IDF as a company commander after finishing his compulsory duty, can give a good 'view from above' of the experiences soldiers go through and how their moral professionalism is tested by hardship of their work:

> I wouldn't use the word boredom, but attrition [*shkhika*] that's the word, if you get tired mentally and physically your ability to fight this war [against attrition] is much smaller. As I said before, I, in this Intifada, didn't stand eight hours at a checkpoint. But who did, I refuse to use the word boredom,

I use *shkhika*, it's a situation that in order to stay normal you have to be *constantly* at war, to stay in your place is to run. You have to fight with yourself not to do it. The easiest way is to go with the flow [*lehisahef*], when there is a person at the checkpoint everyday that can't go in and you tell him again and again, he comes and you tell him to stand at the side and he doesn't do that, what happens at the third time after you didn't sleep for three nights ... to stay sane you have to fight the whole time, the natural way is to be swept into behaviour that is less humane.

Eviatar points out a very crucial point – the ability of attrition and the emotions of soldiers to affect their actual behaviour. In his eyes the real war the soldiers are fighting is within themselves; the struggle to fight the effect of the routine, to fight becoming numb and indifferent. In his words it is thus much harder to behave morally and stay 'sane' than to behave 'less humanely', something he even depicts as 'natural' behaviour. The following quote describes how another commander realizes that he has 'lost' his sanity and how difficult this 'fight' against losing it is:

The minute I saw him [a Palestinian youth who had run away from him several times] I burst at him overwhelmed with rage and hatred I had never experienced before in my life. I grabbed him by the neck, and choked him as I pushed him a few metres towards the pavement, where I bound his hands and feet hard with plastic cuffs until his skin bled, and detained him. All this time the soldiers at the checkpoint were watching – these same soldiers I commanded for over eight months, with whom I served all that time in the Territories, trying to explain how wrong it was to use violence against the Palestinian population, with whom I argued for hours on how immoral it is to puncture car tires, to whom I tried to give a personal example on how important it is to give water to Palestinians who were held at checkpoints on a hot day. All that teaching and personal example went down the drain at this small instant in which I lost my sanity ... This incident made me understand that if such outburst could happen to me – a commander who tried to persuade a whole platoon (soldiers and commanders) how immoral such violent behaviour is – such outbursts must and will have to occur to countless soldiers serving in the Territories in those tough, frustrating, and impossible situations. Indeed I have encountered many cases in which my soldiers and my junior officers behaved abominably towards the Palestinian population. After that incident, when I encountered such a case, I could better understand what the soldiers went through, and how impossible it is to stay sane in these places, and how I hope my sons will not be in the same places, and will not have to fight themselves in order to stay sane.

(BS Maltreatment)

Thus, the struggle against attrition is a very hard one and is not won by many soldiers. Even this commander who viewed himself as very moral, very patient and empathetic to the suffering of the Palestinian population that he and his soldiers dealt with, found himself in a situation of rage and aggression that was very much unlike him.

The explanation the commander gives relates to the 'tough, frustrating, and impossible situations' soldiers face in the Territories. These situations all involve a certain amount of emotional and physical attrition that has a profound effect on the moral reasoning of soldiers and, consequently, on their moral professionalism. Verweij takes this into consideration when she speaks about the aspect of resilience that should be part of morally professional conduct. This resilience should accommodate the soldier's difficult and conflicting emotions, but also make it possible for him to give these emotions a place without turning to violent acts (Verweij 2008: 17). Guy, however, shows understanding for the aggressive behaviour of his soldiers in such circumstances, even though he does not condone it:

> That is one of the reasons that these incidents occurred that were in the grey zone, it's attrition [*shkhika*] in the military is ... they're children in the end, there are no games, children have a certain line till where they can go, so yes, after they haven't seen their girlfriend for more than 3 weeks, I suppose that they can't always control themselves when an Arab worker or child, especially if it's a Arab youth of 18 that says a wrong word, it could be that they will give him a slap in the face.

Yossi relates how some of his soldiers 'lost it' during Operation Defensive Shield:

> There were a lot that broke down, I had a soldier that I think on the last night, 2 o'clock in the night, we were guarding, and suddenly he decides he shoots for no reason, and he took apart a house with bullets. There were a lot of falls of tension, we needed to deal with ... Because of the tension, fear, pressure, suddenly he sees that death is really ... someone fell here, in the company there are dead, there is a chance to get it [to die, *lekabel*].

Behaving in a morally professional manner would mean that they can combat such influences of their work environment. Their ability to recognize moral situations and to deal with them in a morally proper way is tested time and again. Verweij's concept of resilience is important to take into consideration here as it makes clear that behaving in a morally professional way means not only knowing what a moral situation is and combating the external aspects of the difficult work one has to perform, but also being able to deal with moral dilemmas and the emotional difficulties these involve, while giving these emotions a place. As the examples above showed, this is often not the case with Israeli soldiers in the OPT. Soldiers can 'lose it' and sometimes conduct themselves in a violent or harassing manner.

Cognitive Blurring

This numbed moral competency or flawed moral professionalism is accompanied by something I would like to call a state of cognitive blurring. As we have already seen in many quotes from soldiers, the boredom, the cold, the heat, the fear and the power they have all have a profound effect on their behaviour towards the Palestinian civilian population they come into contact with at the checkpoints or during arrests.

Cognitive blurring can be defined as the failure to grasp a meaning or experience cognitively. One does not recognize what is in front of one's eyes as of a certain significance that should be acted upon. When speaking about morality this means that a situation or problem is not recognized as containing a moral dilemma. One fails to see the moral importance because one's moral framework is not triggered (see van Baarda and Verweij 2006: 14). Such a state we could also call a 'moral slumber' (Grossmann 1988: 147) or a state of moral fatigue (Cohen 2001: 192).

The state of cognitive blurring is characterized by a high degree of indifference that is connected to the physical, mental and cognitive numbing discussed above. Soldiers seem not to care about what happens around them, they are indifferent to the suffering of the Palestinians or to the way they are treated. Dar et al. already recognized this state during the First Intifada when during their study 'several respondents reported a blunting of the emotions and indifference, sometimes extending to lack of perception of the surroundings' (Dar et al. 2000: 299).

The following two testimonies of soldiers from an elite paratrooper unit show the ambivalent feelings of the two and the process they went through from having difficulties with the activities of arresting to becoming indifferent to it:

> In short, the arrests, in the end you become indifferent, in the beginning it was very hard for me, you come to arrest someone, there is some kind of indication [intelligence information], if there isn't any indication, what can you do, you do this disgusting job and you wake up in the morning and forget about the contact with the population.
>
> (BS 58-59, translation EG)

> All these arrests, very fast you become indifferent to them. The first time you do an arrest you suddenly see this little kid that's afraid of you and you say 'what, I'm not a scary person', this broke me up, it changed the way I looked at things, you suddenly understand how others see you and this really got to me, but when you have already done a few arrests, you become indifferent to this feeling ... the whole idea is to go home as quickly as possible. From that point of view you get indifferent.
>
> (BS 58–59, translation EG)

Failing to recognize the situation in front of you as morally problematic and failing to feel empathy for the suffering of others can easily lead to aggressive and immoral behaviour toward people or their possessions. Being in a situation where one is worn out (tired, bored, tense, hot or cold) can have a profound effect on the conduct of soldiers, as the following quote shows:

> In the beginning you treat them with more respect, with time you wear out. You start to bother them more ... (Q: 'Where does this come from?') From the boredom, if you're at the checkpoint everyday ... there is nothing you can do. You can be the most humane person around ... there is a lot of boredom, you hold this grudge, you have to be here for the settlers you don't want to be there ... so you take it out on them [the Palestinians]. On whom can you take it out? Not hitting or so, but you tell them 'open the trunk', open this, what do you have here, what do you have there? Also if it's not needed, it's your 'thing' ... like you're at the checkpoint and you have to sit out the time somehow, you have talked to every one of the guys, so you go to them [the Palestinians]. You have these stories, I understand where it's coming from. That there really is harassment. I understand exactly where it comes from. I don't accept it but I understand it.

Yoel remembers a period when he and his soldiers were stationed in the heat of the Gaza Strip, locked up in small military armoured vehicles:

> Listen, one of the games, it's bad, but after a week you are in a Puma [military armoured vehicle] in Gaza, and I didn't do it, but my soldiers did, you are a week in a Puma, you're not allowed to do anything, everyone is on top of each other, in a puma there are supposed to be maximum seven/eight people, we were with thirteen people in a Puma. Everyone shits in their helmets, it's really, really hot, you can't open the sides because they shoot at you all the time, we were there let's say three–four days, and at a certain moment, there is a MAG [automatic weapon] that you can shoot with from within, you don't go outside, so they would play with taking down solar heaters.[46]

In this last example, soldiers are cramped together in small vehicles for days on end with nothing to do but wait. Their commander claims to understand why they 'take it out' on the water containers of the Palestinians living in the surrounding area. Both soldiers and their commander seem oblivious to the suffering they bring to other people with their random acts of shooting, though, a clear example of their blurred view of the reality around them.

---

46. On the roofs of Palestinian houses big black containers can be found in which water is warmed by the sun; these are at times shot at by soldiers.

Detachment: 'Not Thinking About It'

Another issue concerning the moral behaviour of soldiers is the issue of detachment. This distancing from one's experiences will be explored through some concepts used by soldiers when explaining their experiences. A recurring theme in the discourse of Israeli soldiers is that of 'no time to think' or 'not thinking about it'. Such utterances are often connected to the description of situations where there was literally no time to think one's activities over. During arrest operations, but also in the time between activities, everything has to happen as quickly as possible. Many soldiers indicated that because of the little resting time they had, there was no time left to think things over or to think about what they had done just a few hours before.

The fact that soldiers seem to have no time to think about the actions and operations they participate in has an effect on their moral behaviour. When there is no time to think, there is certainly no time to deliberate about one's actions or to take the time to internalize the situation at hand and think about the meaning of one's actions. To illustrate this I will give a few examples.

Oren tells about the time he and his comrades were sent into the Territories as new recruits when the Second Intifada had just broken out. In what he says, a lack of direction in the military activities becomes clear. In the chaos of those first days of the Intifada, no one knew exactly what was going on, the soldiers just seemed to follow their commanders without understanding what was happening around them.

> In the beginning, we didn't think, they [the superiors] didn't understand still what was happening. I don't remember thinking about it, there wasn't time to think. All in all it was quite stressful; no one knew that it would last for so long. They didn't prepare for it. In the beginning it was a chaos, they took us from the base suddenly to Gilo [neighbourhood of Jerusalem that was heavily attacked in the beginning of the Al-Aqsa Intifada], there were rumours but no one knew what was happening.

> In principle a simple soldier isn't supposed to take responsibility on himself. The commander has more experience, more authority. (Q: 'Did the soldiers know/ask what and why things were happening?') There is no time to think, I don't remember that I thought about it, you don't get to go home for a month, we have to run from place to place, there are problems. Maybe after a few months you start to think what did we do and why.

The last example is from Doron, a soldier from an elite unit in the Nahal Brigade who was very reflective about his military duty, which had, in fact, just ended when he was interviewed. Here he puts into words the reasons he believes cause soldiers to become 'animals' that do not think but just do:

It turned me, the military, in many instances into an animal, a stupid one, that doesn't think, the whole issue with the Palestinians, the contact with them, the friction with them, sometimes you do think, because they trained you like that, you don't use your head to see if it's logical or illogical, because if a person with a head on his shoulders would think about all kinds of things during his service, a lot of things would have looked different ... it's bad that there is no thinking, that there is no space for it, and you do turn into a kind of animal. (Q: 'How does this show?') In the operations that you do, the way you speak to people, you speak in a very bad manner to people that are older than you.

Especially the last example, points to the fact that not thinking about one's actions can easily result in misconduct by soldiers. Activities are done in a rush and, as a result, no time is taken to look at the situation, to assess it and to act in a morally professional way.

However, besides it being an actual issue of time, there also seems to be a conscious effort by soldiers not to think about their activities, their feelings and their surroundings too much. When they are 'there', inside the Territories, within their military space, they prefer not to think about what they are doing, because realizing exactly what their actions are and what consequences they might have could make it very difficult for soldiers to carry out those activities.

An expression used when speaking about this 'non-thinking' mode soldiers get into is *rosh katan* (small head).[47] The expression points to the deliberate avoidance of getting too deep into what is happening around you or of using your ability to deliberate. A soldier that has a *rosh katan* does not ask too much about what he is doing and does only what he is told without being interested in the bigger picture of his actions and, thus, without taking any real responsibility for them.

This mechanism of detachment helps soldiers to carry out their work without letting their emotions or rational thoughts get in the way. A soldier who, for example, has to enter a Palestinian house at night will have an easier task if he does not think too much about the inhabitants, about the impact of his actions on them or about his own fear. Such coping mechanisms will be discussed in more detail in the next chapter.

The impression one gets is that the military itself is also interested in soldiers keeping a low profile, following the orders they get without asking questions about the reasons behind these orders. Soldiers who think about their activities and who form their own opinions on what should or should not be done can cause operational difficulties as they will be less inclined to just follow the orders they receive. Keeping soldiers 'dumb' or at least not having them think too much thus safeguards military operational effectiveness. Commanders, however, are expected

---

47. See Ben-Ari 1998 where he discusses the metaphor of the brain used by military personnel when speaking about a unit or brigade.

to *leagdil rosh*, to open their minds, look around them, ask questions and try to understand the context of their activities and orders.

Haggai sees benefits for the soldier himself in not thinking about his actions too much. In his words it saves the soldier from uncertain situations and difficult decision making:

> Yes is yes, no is no. It's black and white, it's the military, the only one who can think is the commander, or the platoon commander, doesn't matter, the one who is leading, he is the only one who can think beyond, soldiers only have yes or no, they don't get space to think. And that actually prevents the entire 'if' and all the 'maybe'. It secures us in that way.

Doron, however, sees some difficulties with not knowing or reflecting upon the situation at hand. By behaving like this, soldiers do not take any responsibility upon themselves and do not show any interest in the situation they are in or in the activities they carry out:

> That's how a soldier looks like, when he's just a soldier, he doesn't have any responsibility, he doesn't demand some responsibility, there are those who say great, who don't want that, they don't want, but there are also soldiers that don't show any interest, they do what they are told and that's it. It ends; no one talks to them until they are going to do something else.

To have a *rosh katan* or 'small head' and to refrain from thinking about one's activities can easily lead to detachment from the situation one is in and to a failure to see the gravity of one's acts or the moral problem at hand.

Zadok puts in words how the situation changes when one becomes a commander. With the responsibility that a commander has, his mind 'opens up' and he starts to reflect on his activities, thus being able to make the moral distinction between right and wrong:

> As a soldier I was with my head against the wall. What I saw everyone do, I did. As a commander you understand more, as a soldier you say, you see the commander do like that, then I'll also do it. Don't think too much, *rosh katan*. That's the purpose of the military. When you're a commander, when you have responsibility, you start looking more, at the different directions, what can happen if this, then you already start to think differently, and see that what you do is not right. But you can't say I'm sorry, you can't say excuse me; you did it, that's it.

To act in a morally responsible way and to be morally competent or morally professional, one needs to think. A person will have to think about the situation he finds himself in, view it within its context and decide on the best way to act. 'Not thinking' increases the chances of misbehaviour by soldiers and does not give them the opportunity to reflect on their actions. The soldiers fail to recognize what they see in front of them or to see their own actions as morally problematic; their moral framework is not triggered. In her analysis of Hannah Arendt's work, Verweij points to this issue and writes: '[R]esponsibility and accountability are the manifestation of the ability to think, i.e. of the ability to conduct this inner dialogue, an ability that can be developed by everybody' (Verweij 2002: 156).

One of the soldiers quoted above even goes as far as to say that a soldier can become a 'sort of animal' from this lack of thinking, an animal that just acts without giving these acts a thought. Other metaphors about soldiers becoming robots were also used, pointing to the prevalence of acting without thinking.

In Retrospect

In the last quote, the soldier in question talks about looking back in retrospect and understanding how certain things he had done were not right. Zigon has called the moments that one 'has to stop and consider how to act or to be morally appropriate' ethics (2008: 164). I would say the same is true when reflecting on activities in retrospect. This is an important notion here; while most activities by soldiers were at that time done 'without thinking', relating about these experiences afterwards is a reflective moment in which this behaviour is reassessed by the actor. In the quote above this process of 'doing ethics' was, according to Zadok, related to becoming a commander and, as such, becoming more centrally involved in the activities of his unit and the military as a whole. Other soldiers have declared that after being released from the military for a while, the distance in time and often also space (young Israelis flock abroad in large numbers after their release from the military)[48] allows them to look back and understand more deeply what their activities entailed, how many risks they took and what the impact of their actions was on the people involved.

In relation to reinforcing a curfew, Golan, for example, talks about how he would explain his actions to Palestinians. Believing at first that they just did not understand how the military system worked, he then comes to an understanding that he, at the time, was the one who did not understand what was really going on. The people he stopped just wanted to go to work without feeling the need to understand the Israeli military system:

> We tell them, we are here, I don't like taking the air out of your tyres but I do this so you will tell your cousin, that's how we talk to them, for sure. And they say 'yes, yes'. Then I thought well they don't understand, they don't see

---

48. See the documentary *Flipping Out* by Yoav Shamir about the problematic issue of drug use during such trips.

the institutional view, now I see, goddamn, the guy wants to go to work, I didn't understand.

Sitting besides the pool in a quiet *kibbutz*, Doron talks about how he cannot understand how he did the things he did as a soldier. Today, after thinking and realizing how many risks he took, he says he would 'die of fear' if he had to do it again:

> No, in the Territories they release you, it's amazing, the thought, suddenly I say, when I was sitting with my friends in the *kibbutz* and I say if today I was going to run with a weapon over there in a refugee camp, I would die of fear. And then I did it all the time, and in the military they also teach you not to think, whatever they tell you, you do. Doesn't interest you ... whenever they tell you 'go' [*kadima*] ... But now, you're in civilian life, you know what you have to lose, and what you leave behind. It's much more difficult.

The fact that after the release of soldiers from their service many realize their actions could have been more considerate and less harsh emphasizes the influence their detachment from the situation they were in had on their actual behaviour as soldiers. Not thinking about one's actions because of lack of time or because of conscious distancing enhances the state of moral numbing soldiers find themselves in.

Conclusion

In the above quotes soldiers voice their understanding of the behaviour of their comrades. It is clear to them that when you find yourself in such a situation of stress, work overload and attrition, you will do things that you should not. The mental and physical numbing that has been described in the previous chapters, the numbing of the soldiers' moral competence and the cognitive blurring and detachment it can lead to influence the way soldiers see the 'other' and, in particular, treat the 'other'. The power bestowed on them, furthermore, gives them the opportunity to act upon their state of numbness by carrying out senseless acts such as shooting at solar heaters or shouting at Palestinians for no good reason.

The processes of numbing that take place within the different dimensions that were discussed earlier, the emotional, physical and the cognitive, were shown to lead to a state of numbing in the moral dimension: indifference and apathy take over as the principal attitudes of the soldiers. This numbing was linked to the issue of cognitive blurring; the circumstances around the soldiers did not trigger their moral frameworks anymore. Soldiers' detachment from their surroundings was, then, discussed – the conscious and unconscious effort made not to think or to internalize what goes on around them.

These processes all contribute to behaviour that can be aggressive, humiliating or even violent towards the 'other', in this case the Palestinian civilians. It thus has an important impact on their moral decision making, on whether they recognize moral dilemmas as such and, if they do, on the way they deal with them.

In the next chapter I will deal with the moral strategies soldiers use in their discourse, which is formed within the space of their work, under the circumstances already discussed. I will examine several mechanisms and explanations used by soldiers when speaking about their activities and their decision making.

CHAPTER 7

MORALITY IN SPEECH
Discursive Strategies of Soldiers

When people recount their experiences, when they get the opportunity to talk about what they have seen and been through, we end up with accounts. These accounts are highly individual and subjective and this is the reason they have the potential to give us an insight into how people think. Most importantly, though, they can give us insights into the specific ways people speak about their past experiences and thus the way they understand them and want us to understand them. When such experiences and the behaviour of the speaker are complex and ambiguous by nature, and especially when they involve others and thus gain a moral dimension, certain discursive strategies are used to explain or justify them.

In this chapter I will look at the accounts given by Israeli soldiers of their experiences and behaviour during their service in the OPT and I will try to distil from these the dominant discursive strategies used to justify, legitimize or deny this behaviour.

Before getting to these strategies, however, it is important to stress from what point of view these soldiers are being looked at. As mentioned before, within the context of the OPT and the activities of Israeli soldiers, these soldiers can be defined as perpetrators. They are the ones in power after all and they are the ones who execute the acts of violence and harassment that have been discussed here. Being in this position of power, a subject that has been discussed earlier, gives soldiers a certain degree of freedom of action to control other people (in this case, the Palestinians) using different means of verbal or physical aggression. Their sheer presence as an occupying force is enough to create a great inequality in terms of freedom and power. This is not to say that all Israeli soldiers serving within the OPT are perpetrators of actual atrocities or crimes of war. But acts do not have to be of great importance to create a victim and hence a perpetrator. The language and discursive techniques of aggressors in general are similar and the discourses of justification, legitimization and denial are comparable. In this chapter I will, then, examine the speech of soldiers when they explain, legitimize, rationalize or deny their actions.

Looking at the actual language that soldiers use can help us understand their discursive strategies. Issues at hand will include the important repertoires that come up when soldiers explain their behaviour during their service, what dominant strategies are used and the extent to which soldiers acknowledge the suffering they witness and actively perpetrate. Only when we look at the accounts that soldiers give about their acts can we see how they distinguish between right and wrong behaviour and what their moralities actually look like. Some of the repertoires that have been distilled from the language of soldiers and that will be discussed here are passivity, professionalism and ideological justifications.

It is important to note that the themes and strategies that will be discussed are the dominant themes that were found in the soldiers' discourses. There is a very rich range of discursive strategies and not all can be discussed here, however. For this reason, the dominant themes and strategies that were found to be reoccurring in the interviews were chosen for further exploration. Such strategies are often interconnected and combined by the speakers and can be simultaneously used in one and the same conversation.

On the surface, Israeli soldiers seem to take a passive stance towards the situation they find themselves in as soldiers serving in the Occupied Palestinian Territories, carrying out an occupation and as controllers of another people. As we shall see later, utterances such as 'There is nothing I can do', 'You have to do it' and 'You have to do your job' are abundant in their accounts. The occupation of the Territories by the Israeli military stays relatively unquestioned by the soldiers, being taken as a given, as a situation they cannot change and within which they need to work due to factors beyond their control. Even though exceptions exist, the soldiers who did question the occupation and their role within it continued to serve and to follow the orders given to them. Their critical opinions were given by them as civilians; as soldiers they did their job without asking too many questions or resisting the orders they received.[49]

Soldiers' Talk

Seu argues that the (psychological) explanations given by people and the discourse they use around the confrontation with the suffering of others can be seen as constructions of accounts and justifications (Seu 2003). The 'talk' of people should be seen as a form of social action and, as such, explanations given by people are very important when trying to understand human behaviour. The fact that Seu takes theories from critical discursive psychology as her framework is of interest because

---

49. Especially during the Lebanon War of 1982–83 this attitude of (reserve) soldiers was manifested for the first time in an explicit form; these soldiers would fight during the week and protest against the war in the weekends at demonstrations for Peace Now. This was also known as the 'Shoot and Cry' phenomenon. Today such activism is far away from most serving soldiers although some still have critical ideas.

critical psychologists 'are much more interested in the way people construct and reconstruct the world and their subjectivity in everyday talk' (Seu 2003: 190), an approach I would like to use here.

Seu's ideas about how to look at people's daily explanations and her use of psychological theories are useful when looking at the discourse of Israeli soldiers in the field. The 'talk' of the soldiers should indeed be seen as a site for constructing accounts and hence the importance of investigating the way they talk, explain and justify their actions and behaviour. Looking at the way discourse is constructed and not only at the message of the speaker is what is important here.

Moreover, it is important to pay attention to the 'agentic' role a soldier gives himself within the account of his experiences. As we shall see shortly, many Israeli soldiers do not use the 'I' form but the passive 'you' when they are talking about their own personal experiences.[50] For instance, a soldier will say 'and then you go into that house' instead of 'and then I went into that house'. The use of a passive agent is important in the way it creates distance between the actual action and the agent himself. Bandura even warns about the use of the 'agentless passive voice' (2002: 105) according to which acts are carried out by nameless forces such as when 'the truck drove into the crowd'. The driver of the truck remains absent and thus innocent here.

In Maoz's work on the First Intifada, she makes a distinction between 'ambivalents' and 'legitimizers' when talking about the mechanisms soldiers use during asymmetrical encounters with Palestinian civilians (Maoz 2001). Soldiers in the first category were, thus, ambivalent about the use of force in clashes with Palestinians while the latter group legitimized it. In this work a similar tendency was found. Although most interviewees fell within the ambivalent category there were, however, as we shall see, also soldiers who legitimized their violent activities towards Palestinians and who did not admit any ambivalence.

The Minimization of Moral Agency

As mentioned before, from initial conversations with soldiers a sense of 'accepting passivity' or a lack of agency was noticed when they spoke about their presence and activities in the OPT. They took the occupation of the OPT by the IDF as a given and no questions were asked relating to reasons or explanations concerning the often unclear situations they found themselves in. Even when the suffering and hardship of Palestinians that they witnessed were recognized as such, they did not generate any kind of responsive action. This passive stance could be called a minimization of their agentive role (Bandura 2002: 106), meaning that distance is taken from the suffering that is witnessed and

---

50. With thanks to Avichay Sharon of Breaking the Silence who pointed this out to me.

responsibility is evaded or displaced (ibid.). The issues related to such a stance are: inaction, apathy, indifference and feelings of helplessness, all of which feature in the discourse of the soldiers. Besides being insensitive or indifferent to the suffering of others, a lack of agency could also mean a sense of being unable to do something while still acknowledging the pain of others.

'Ma La'asot' (*What can You Do?*) or 'Ein Ma La'asot' (*There is Nothing You can Do*)

> In the [Gaza] strip it's also intensive. (Q: 'What did you do?') [Worked on D9 (bulldozer)] we were in the area of Netzarim, at the entrance of Netzarim. There were shootings and explosives on buses; 200 metres from the road they cleared everything. Houses, groves, everything. Except for one mosque, they didn't touch it. It was like a flat plate. So we took down houses and olive trees. (Q: 'How did you feel?') You know for an Arab what is important is first of all his olive trees. After that come his wife and the house. It's not nice, I started to do some gardening,[51] so it's not nice, but we had to do it, *what can you do*. It would happen anyway.
>
> (emphasis added)

In the language Israeli soldiers use, *Ein ma la'asot* or *Ma la'asot* ('There is nothing you can do / What can you do?') is a frequently recurring theme. Soldiers use it especially when confronted with situations they see as problematic or painful, such as those involving the suffering of Palestinian civilians whose houses they invade or whose groves they destroy, as seen in the quote above. Often such phrases are added after a description of an operation in which civilians were involved. The soldier then typically talks about the operation he participated in, in an unemotional manner, adds information about the civilians that were present, for example a family in a house that was entered at night for a search, and finishes with the sentence: 'There is nothing you can do'. In such accounts, where activities are carried out in groups, the division of tasks diffuses responsibility. Attention is given by the speaker to the factual details of the operation and not so much to its meaning and actual consequences (Bandura 2002: 107).

When we look more closely at the moral strategy that is used here we can first see that the soldier acknowledges the suffering of the others, or at least their discomfort. Then, however, he goes on to state that this is out of his hands; the work has to be done and as such it is morally justified (Bandura 2002). That there is some suffering involved seems

---

51. Michael explained in this interview how he took up gardening as a hobby, thus allowing him to understand the connection of the Palestinians to their groves and trees more deeply.

unavoidable. As Michael says in the above quote: 'It would happen anyway'. This strategy is a typical example of what Cohen calls 'implicatory' denial. As mentioned before, within this type of denial the general interpretation of an act is acknowledged but responsibility for it is not taken. Its moral implications are interpreted as unimportant, untrue or exaggerated.

In the following example, Liron, a *kibbutz* member from the centre of the country who served in the Nahal 50 Battalion and who was trained as a sniper,[52] talks about his experiences at checkpoints in the OPT. From this quote we can conclude that he feels strongly that checkpoints exist for a good reason, even though the work linked to them was not always easy:

> There, you really feel you have to be there. You check trucks and cars and what can you do, they are all potentials.[53] So we check the car, we don't turn everything upside down, check it like we are supposed to ... It's not like you take this guy into an alley and beat him up. You don't do things like that, there is always a reason ... you do what you have to and let the guy go. In Bethlehem and Hebron, sometimes there were sudden checkpoints that we put up and we had to stop people, also in the entrance to Jerusalem. There was a taxi that passed and there was a woman that had a miscarriage and they took the foetus with them to bury in the village, and one of my friends had to check the box. These are instances that there is nothing you can do.

Liron emphasizes that he and his comrades were never brutal 'for no reason'; if they were forceful it meant they had a reason to be. He senses the difficulty of the situation when a soldier has to stop a woman at the checkpoint with her lifeless child in order to check her. However, it is clear from his words that he feels that the inspections these Palestinians are subjected to are justified, difficult as they may be for the Palestinians and even for the soldiers. Again, we come upon a form of moral disengagement, as Bandura calls it, in the form of moral justification within which the role of the perpetrator in the harm caused is minimized and 'pernicious conduct is made personally and socially acceptable' (Bandura 2002: 103).

When Nir, another *kibbutz* member who served in the Nahal 50 Battalion, talks about working in a so-called 'straw widow', he describes the situation as difficult for the soldiers from a few different perspectives. But, he adds, 'the situation made it necessary', in other words there was nothing else he and his comrades could do, the situation they were in made it impossible for them to act otherwise:

---

52. The Nahal 50 Battalion traditionally consists of members of *kibbutzim* and *moshavim*, small agricultural settlements generally with a more leftist political outlook. Members have the reputation of behaving in a more moral way towards Palestinians.
53. By 'potentials' this soldier means possible terrorists – the passers-by could all potentially be suicide bombers or they could be aiding a terrorist attack.

It was hard, it wasn't easy, from a mental perspective, from a physical perspective, and also if you sleep in a house with all your things on you, you don't sleep well. You spend a few hours there and then you go back into the field, that's hard. But the situation made it necessary it was like, there is nothing you can do [*ein ma la'asot*], this is the necessity, the situation, we need it. It's either us or them at the moment. It's the black and white, either us or them, there aren't a lot of options.

Using sentences like 'There is nothing you can do' or 'What can I do?' seems to indicate the feeling the soldiers have that the situation is out of their hands; they cannot change it in any way. This feeling can, of course, indicate a real lack of power to change a certain situation but it can also be imagined or evoked by the soldiers in an effort to distance themselves from taking any responsibility. In the perception of the soldiers, the situation is acknowledged and the suffering or hardship involved is not denied. However, the situation comes from a necessity (such as security considerations) and as such their actions within it are perceived to be justified. The theme of self-defence is also used here ('It's either them or us'), which enhances the feeling of the soldiers that they have no other choice but to act as they do. It is very clear that the soldiers take no responsibility whatsoever for their actions or the situations they find themselves in. Again, a case of implicatory denial (Cohen 2001) is at play; suffering and the activities causing it are acknowledged but responsibility is not taken.

In both quotes it also becomes clear that, while acknowledging the suffering or the difficult situation of the Palestinians, the real difficulty the soldiers speak of is the difficulty they themselves have as witnesses or as reluctant instigators of this suffering. Here, part of the blame for having to perpetrate harmful activities is, surprisingly, given to the victims. Because of their presence as a generalized entity, as Palestinians, as 'the other', the soldiers have to do what they do (Bandura 2002: 110).

Lo Na'im *(Not Nice)*

Often the phrase 'It's not nice' (the expression *lo na'im*) is added to phrases like 'There is nothing you can do'. This expression is used as: 'It's not nice, but there is nothing you can do'. The theme of *lo na'im*' demonstrates an acknowledgement on the part of the soldier of the suffering or hardship he has caused or witnessed. However, followed by *ein ma la'asot* (what can you do) this acknowledgment stands on its own with the soldier using the expression taking no responsibility for the situation. Furthermore, we should not confuse this for a sign of guilt or remorse. It is more a statement of acknowledgement and a subsequent acceptance of the situation as it is.

The concept of *Lo na'im* also conveys the reluctance of soldiers to do the work they have to do. They are not proud of their work (earlier labelled as 'dirty work' [Hughes 1958]), work that society and often the workers themselves identify as being less worthy than other work because it literally involves dirt or because of its moral taint. Carrying out activities that are 'not nice' within the military context certainly fulfils the criteria for being dirty work.

However, the hardship or suffering witnessed or caused seems, in the eyes of the soldiers, merely a necessary evil within this dirty work that the soldiers have to carry out. In the following quote Offer, a former soldier from a naval commando unit, expresses his opinion on the humaneness of the IDF. He acknowledges that the operations carried out by the Israeli military are hard for the Palestinian population (or 'not nice', as he phrases it) but, all in all, he wants to make it clear that the Israeli military is a very humane military, too humane even, a clear case of implicatory denial (Cohen 2001):

> We, I don't know about other units, we are humane, and even too humane. We treat them ... And no one comes and shoots at children, and not at women and old people and also men that ... like you don't like a guy and you shoot his foot to shut him up. There is no such thing. Women and children, we even don't bind their hands or eyes. We give a chair to the old people, so they can sit outside. Of course it's not a nice thing, imagine someone coming to your house and saying go outside and they search your house. I understand the population doesn't like it [*lo na'im la*], and of course they don't understand me that I don't want a terrorist to blow himself up in my house tomorrow or in Tel Aviv. But that is the 'best of two evils' I have to do it. So we tell them to get out outside, we tell them to take their shirt up, to lower their pants, not like in a humiliating way, but because there were instances of suicide bombers. And also women and also like you saw on television probably, a child of 15 with explosives. We also don't tell them to take their underwear off or anything, only the pants. Even though I have heard they have made underwear with explosives ... So on one side it's not nice [*lo jafe*] and I think we are humane anyway, we could also say 'take down your pants and underwear' and also to women and humiliate them completely. But we don't do such a thing.

Offer is clearly what Maoz has termed a 'legtimizer' (2001), someone who justifies violent behaviour towards Palestinians and who denies illegal violent actions by the IDF. What is made apparent from this example is a feeling that 'it could be worse', in the sense that the soldiers acknowledge the fact that their actions are harmful to others but not nearly as harmful as others' actions. This strategy is related to what Bandura calls advantageous comparison, where the way 'behaviour is viewed is coloured by what it is compared against' (2002: 105). When you contrast your actions with other, much more severe, actions, your actions will not look as bad. In this case, the behaviour of the soldiers is compared with how they could have behaved.

It could even be possible that the very act of acknowledging such suffering helps soldiers in their efforts to legitimize their own and their comrades' actions for the outside world and their own self-image. When they recognize the suffering of the 'other', this at least makes them human beings (or humane) even if they are the ones inflicting this suffering. The language of soldiers seems to be filled with oppositions such as 'it's not nice, but we have to do it', which in fact direct the issue of responsibility away from the soldiers and puts them in a relatively positive light, since they at least acknowledge the hardship they cause.

Yariv, who as we saw earlier claims to have more leftist ideas than most other soldiers, tells of how during specific activities that he perceived to be particularly superfluous or unfair, he wanted to be present in order to carry them out in a 'good manner' or in his words 'with a smile':

> That is let's say you walk in their market or on the main road and you stop people, just people that seem suspicious to you, and ask them where they are going and what they are doing. And that's it; here I think it's most important to show, to do it with a smile and to do it ... (Q: 'So it was important for you to be there?') Yes that was always important to me to be there to be in charge of ... that was also something that wasn't nice to do. And in my opinion also something that is superfluous, but okay, what can I do.

Different than the other soldiers quoted above, Yariv admits that he perceives activities such as randomly stopping and checking people on the streets to be superfluous and unnecessary. However, standing firmly within the military framework, he uses a form of implicatory denial when he adds 'What can I do?' to indicate that in his view he has no other choice but to follow the orders given to him by his superiors. The only thing he could do, as a minor form of 'resistance', was to be present, behave properly and have his soldiers do the same.

Indifference

Up until now, almost all the examples given showed soldiers who in some way or another were troubled by the suffering they witnessed, even if they legitimized it. However, what we can also find are soldiers who are indifferent to any hardship or distress felt by the Palestinian population. In the following example from a testimony collected by Breaking the Silence, a soldier explains how his service in Hebron was marked by orders that he would execute without asking questions:

> I admit that Hebron is not divisible into periods, for me, it's like one long line. As far as I was concerned, I wasn't sensitive enough to it at the time, to when curfews were imposed, when curfews were lifted. It only affected me when I would go on guard-duty. All I knew was that before going

on guard-duty ... I'd ask: is there a curfew? Is there no curfew? There's a
curfew? Cool, I'll enforce it. No curfew? Cool, be on your way. Most of the
time there was a curfew.

(BS Hebron)

This indifference does not mean that the soldier was not sensitive in
any way to the situation of the Palestinians who were affected by the
curfews he mentioned, but rather that he chose not to be concerned with
it and to just literally follow the rules. Here we see a form of numbing
that has already been discussed earlier, a numbing that results in sheer
detachment and indifference.

Cohen adds another facet to the notion of indifference; when one
does not fully realize the immorality of one's actions, this also falls
under indifference. The acts someone performs are then neutralized and
normalized because everyone is doing it, without having any other (ideological) motives (Cohen 2001: 100).

On a different level, a sense of indifference can also come from a
bigger entity than one soldier or a unit. As Cohen shows us, when a
whole society uses collective denial and activities are thus performed
within a moral vacuum, there is no possibility of seeing that one's actions
are morally wrong (Cohen 2001: 10–11). In the case of the Israeli military this is an important point as many of the activities of the soldiers
are legitimized under the cover of 'security'. By a (self-chosen) lack of
deep knowledge of the situation these activities are, furthermore, often
approved by the Israeli public. Israeli soldiers, then, find themselves in a
situation within which, because of normalization, they cannot (or only
with very great difficulty) make out if their actions are morally wrong
or not.

The strategies covered by the theme of the minimization of moral
agency such as implicatory denial, moral justification, advantageous
comparison and displacement of responsibility are, thus, from one point
of view characterized by acknowledgement of the difficulties Palestinian
civilians go through on a daily basis as a result of the Israeli occupation of the OPT and the operations of the IDF. From another point of
view, however, there is a deep passive acceptance of the situation as it
is, no responsibility is taken and no change is pursued. This acceptance,
combined with a feeling of being unable to change the situation, can be
based on the positioning of the soldiers within a hierarchical situation
with not much room for manoeuvre. However, it is also used by soldiers
to divert responsibility away from themselves. For when you are in a
situation you are unable to change, as they argue they are, even if you
want to, you can hardly be taken to be responsible for it. Furthermore,
the perception of the soldiers (and often the whole society) that their
activities are legitimate and necessary for the greater good (security of
the state) also contributes to the diversion of responsibility elsewhere.

Professionalism (*Miktsoayut*)

(Q: 'Would there be talk about political ideas among the soldiers?') Not so much, more also, there are different opinions, that's obvious, but the moment the operation starts everyone forgets everything, everyone knows that you have to do exactly what is needed, you don't take it into the operations, you try not to deal with it, you know that you will do what you need to do. Also if it goes against your opinions.

Using a discourse of professionalism to explain their behaviour comes very naturally to soldiers. Besides using the actual term for professionalism, '*miktsoayut*', soldiers use many related terms while explaining their actions and decision making in the field. I will make a distinction between two different levels in soldiers' discourse within which the overarching theme of professionalism is used. The first one is the 'bottom-up' approach that a soldier uses when talking about and explaining in his own words his direct behaviour and surroundings. The second level entails a more strategic discourse used by soldiers, but more often by their commanders, within which more general and strategic considerations are made.

The reason for this division is that soldiers, even after their discharge, have a tendency to 'slip back' into the military or strategic discourse that they used during their years of service, which is much more impersonal then their 'normal' discourse. Instead of taking such a strategic discourse to be unauthentic or the opposite (taking the daily talk of soldiers as unreliable), I think it is important to look at both in terms of their own value. When an interviewee suddenly changes the tone of his speech and begins to speak in professional terms about an operation that he participated in, it teaches us a lot about the role such discourse plays in the world of thought of this interviewee. When being asked questions about his service, his memory is directed back to that period and, with this, his language can change.

Instead of treating both levels simultaneously, I have divided them into two levels in order to emphasize their difference. We should not forget, however, that soldiers at times used both levels simultaneously in the same conversation or even the same sentence, and that the division made is thus purely for reasons of clarification.

Bottom-up: Soldiers' Talk

The type of speech that is referred to here could also be called a layman's perception of the activities that soldiers perform in the OPT. Furnham defines this term (which he developed within several contexts, such as psychology, medicine and economics) as 'implicit, informal, "non-scientific" explanations' of 'certain behavioural phenomena' (Furnham 1988: 1). While this approach is used in most parts of this research, it is important to emphasize it explicitly here when we compare it to the more strategic language used by soldiers.

It's a Job / Doing it Right / Doing a Good Job

In the discourse of soldiers, their perception of their activities as 'a job' is striking. This, first of all, tells us a lot about the status that they give their work and, second, it naturalizes their military activities. The activities of the soldiers become ordinary performances without extraordinary meanings. Furthermore, perceiving military work as just a job can point to the use of a discourse of professionalism as a legitimizing factor. When in this frame of mind, then, the work the soldier performs is a job he has to do without having any real say in the matter. To use Cohen's work again, such a strategy could be called a form of interpretative denial, where the facts are acknowledged but their meaning is neutralized.

In addition, a clear displacement of responsibility is at play as the job is usually done to respond to an order given by someone else, someone who should then take responsibility for its consequences. To illustrate the use of the idea of 'it's a job' I will give a few examples of how it is used:

> I'm a person who wants to be professional, I'm not there to make peace, I'm there to do my job. So if someone wants to pass the checkpoint and he's not supposed to pass there and he has 3 boxes of cigarettes, I could professionally say I won't check all the boxes one by one. But I want to make a statement, so I let this guy sit for an hour and a half and I check every box, because explosives can be found in anything and show him I'm not playing games. We check everything and that through this checkpoint no terrorist will go through, here there will be no mistakes. They can go through another section but here it won't happen. So people come with vegetables and we search all the coconuts and through all the lettuce, to make sure a tomato is a tomato.

Golan explicitly uses the actual term of professionalism in this example. As a commander in the artillery, he sees himself as a professional and speaks in terms of 'doing his job' and 'not making peace', making clear he is there to carry out his mission as given to him by decision makers above him. Golan was proud of being very thorough in his work, thorough to the point that his soldiers complained to him about it. He aimed to be a professional and this meant focusing on his mission; making sure that his checkpoint would deter terrorists from attempting to cross it while simultaneously setting an example for his soldiers.

When asked if any explanation was given to the soldiers for the situation in the Territories during the beginning of the Second Intifada, Haggai, who served in Nahal 50, indicated that the explanation given was the following: 'This is the situation, this is what we have to do, and there is no political explanation. A platoon commander comes and does his job and the soldiers the same'.

In short, the reasoning used by Haggai's supervisors was also that there is a job to do and that this is all that needs to be known. Their message was that the soldiers should not look at the political side of what they are doing; they, as soldiers, should follow their orders, do their work and nothing more. This clearly facilitates a distance between the soldier and the consequences that his activities have. The situation is simplified for the soldiers, being diminished to 'just performing the job', diffusing responsibility for the consequences and decision making concerning this job to the upper echelons. It is another example of implicatory denial as defined by Cohen (2001).

Reminiscing about his service as a D9 (big bulldozer) operator in the Gaza Strip, Michael remembers his initial reluctance to do this work. After destroying the first house, however, the work became easier, 'just another job' without any room for deliberation: 'What, I'm going to destroy someone's house? After that, a house, another house, another house.' (Q: 'And afterwards?') 'It is work, you have to do it. If everyone would think and do whatever he wanted ...'

Bandura indicates how moral disengagement is often not a direct process but rather something that evolves in steps. After the first act, it becomes easier to take the next step and to then perform even more serious acts without one's moral self-censure acting as an effective break (Bandura 2002: 110). The example above shows this clearly.

When it comes to communication with outsiders (for example, Palestinians, reporters or activists) about certain military activities, Nir is very clear: 'We come and do our jobs, there is no use in talking to them, there are very clear things we have to do, there is no use in discussing things'.

Elsewhere he says: 'We want to do our job, questions and stuff can go to the government, to the one who is responsible, we are not ... not with us. I'm not a minister or ... I don't have any decision, I execute [orders]'. When there is a job to do, Nir seems to say, there is no benefit in discussing or explaining; a job has to be done and that is all there is to it. Questions can go 'up' to the ones who are responsible; he himself is not responsible for the actions he is carrying out. Golan gives the same sort of explanation: he distances himself from the decision makers of the state and, thus, from taking responsibility: 'Like a checkpoint, it annoys the population and then you need more checkpoints, but in the end this is the military's job, so it is with the state then, but I'm not with the state, I'm in the military. So the sergeant, 19-years-old, has to understand the state's decision'.

In short, when using phrases such as 'I'm just doing my job' or 'it's a job', Israeli soldiers use a professional discourse that describes their military activities as 'normal' jobs. This normalization, furthermore, gives them the opportunity to distance themselves from the activities they carry out. Responsibility for action and its consequences is displaced and its meanings are neutralized. When someone says he is 'just doing his job' in this context, the performer does not seem to take responsibility for this job and the way it is carried out; people higher up gave him the orders and hence he is not the one who should be held responsible or who should even be obliged to explain his actions.

As Good as Possible

Just as soldiers see their work as 'just a job', their goal is to do this job as 'well as they can'. This fits neatly within the professional discourse that is discussed here: the job has to be done smoothly, as fast and thoroughly as possible. As noticed before, this means maintaining order at the checkpoint, having as little contact with Palestinian civilians as possible and adopting a professional attitude as a soldier. While having a distinct professional character, there is also a moral element to these explanations. The behaviour of soldiers should also be as good as possible and, thus, as humane as possible. This latter characterization will be the focus here. Bandura calls this a form of inhibitive moral agency, which means 'the power to refrain from behaving inhumanely', as opposed to proactive agency, which means the 'power to behave humanely' (Bandura 2002: 111). Both notions can help us understand the meaning of trying to behave as well as one can while not actually adjusting one's activities in order to behave in a more moral manner.

Omer, who served in an elite unit of the paratroopers, gives a good example of this notion when he speaks of the preparation he and his comrades received before performing arrest operations. He does not speak about changing the way the work is done, but merely about how he can refrain from behaving in a bad or immoral way while doing his usual job:

> Specific for an operation; then they tell you how to treat people, not to do things that aren't allowed, to behave well, all the purity of arms and things like that they go through it a lot because a lot of times you get in a situation where you have to use your weapon, and point at people, all the time they say to use as little force as possible, only when there is danger and then not overuse it. A weapon for example is something that you're not allowed to use at all, not to shoot in the air, only if you have to.

In the following quote, Omer emphasizes how an operation that is carried out should 'look good' in the eyes of others. He does not specify who these others are and who will judge the soldiers afterwards, though; they could be the outside world in general, the media or the public, for example. It is clear, however, that 'looks' are important for soldiers and the military in general. We could call this the importance of an external 'gaze'; of the power and control observers have on performers within a certain arena, for example a checkpoint: 'Because in the end that is the professional, in an arrest that's how they will see us afterwards, in the stakeouts, everything will look better'.

Interrelated with carrying out a job as well as possible is, then, the notion of behaving as well as possible, or 'to hurt as little as possible'. Soldiers who use these notions are referring to the efforts they make to do their jobs as efficiently as they can without unnecessarily hurting the Palestinian civilians who they are confronted with. Behaving as well as possible during a military operation without hurting or upsetting the lives of Palestinian civilians too much is considered a prerequisite for being professional. A soldier comes to do his job, to carry out a specific operation or specific orders and no more than that. Unnecessary harm or harassment is seen as unprofessional and unproductive conduct and should, therefore, be avoided.

This kind of inhibitive agency is part of the more general military notion of minimizing collateral damage. Operations are, therefore, carried out in such a way as to cause as few civilian casualties as possible, always taking such casualties into account. The phrase collateral damage is, furthermore, a classic example of what Bandura calls euphemistic labelling: neutralizing your activities by the use of language that hides the fact that these cause people to die (Bandura 2002).

We should add here that the definition of harassment or unnecessary harm is not clear-cut. What for an outsider might seem superfluous violent behaviour could be very legitimate in the eyes of a soldier. However, what is important here is the notion that soldiers themselves have that their work should be carried out professionally and that, hence, their behaviour towards Palestinian civilians should be 'as good as possible'. Again the image of a unit or platoon is important here; it is important for the soldiers to be seen as professionals within the gaze of outsiders.

In the next example, Omer explains how he treated Palestinians during arrest operations. He emphasizes several times that his unit made an effort to treat people with the utmost respect, adding that this should, however, never affect the necessary use of force itself. Treating people with respect and hurting them as little as possible was, then, limited by the safety considerations of the soldiers. Nonetheless, from what he says, it becomes obvious that a real effort was made by him and his comrades to perform their work as smoothly and respectfully as possible:

I don't know how it is in other units, but we would take care all the time to behave well and for example we do an arrest and take the head of the house [*baál habait*], we don't do it in front of the family, we take him aside so they won't see. So there won't be hysteria. We separate the women from the men, also if you want to check that he doesn't have explosives on him, then every man that comes out of the house you tell him [in Arabic] take up your shirt, take down your pants, to check that there isn't something there. So first of all you take the men aside so it won't be in front of the women, and not in front of the children, as much as possible yes, so far as it doesn't endanger the force. Because with them the honour [*kavod*] is very important, to tell the head of the house to take down his pants in front of his daughters that's really ... that really hurts their honour [*kavod*]. We try not to do this, to take them to the side, also on the issue of honour is that all the time they tell us not to touch their belongings in the house, the lights you have to turn on, you have no choice, sometimes you don't have a choice, there are houses you have to turn upside down if they say there are weapons inside, what can you do, then you turn the house upside down, but we try not to break things, but to try to keep their privacy as much as possible, to take care of their property, to hurt as little as possible, to damage [*lehazik*] as little as possible.

In summary, doing a good job, without any soldiers getting hurt and with a minimum of suffering on the Palestinian side, is perceived to be an important part of soldiers' professional conduct. This emphasizes good behaviour, which has as its goal to reflect positively on the soldiers when outsiders are scrutinizing them. Behaving properly, however, is limited by the safety considerations of the soldiers and seems to have an instrumental character.

Following Orders

Not surprisingly, 'following orders' is an often recurring theme in the interviews with soldiers. This was one of the influential 'normative orders' (Herbert 1997) influencing their reality. Soldiers everywhere, at all times in history, have learned that one of the most important skills they should master is that of following orders, preferably without asking too many questions. This notion was already touched on when I discussed the 'small head' (*rosh katan*) theme earlier. From the examples above, this repertoire could already be deciphered. Again and again soldiers point to the fact that they were ordered to perform the tasks that they characterize as 'a job' and can therefore not be expected to take responsibility for them.

Responsibility is very clearly displaced to different parties, mostly upwards to commanders or even the state. Important here is the location of agency: who does what and who takes responsibility for the actions carried out? Trust is put in the commanders to give the correct and legitimate orders to their soldiers as the latter do not see the situation from the 'system's point of view' (a notion that will be discussed shortly) and thus have to rely on the knowledge of their superiors.

Following orders, then, is for many soldiers closely related to their lack of ability to deliberate on their activities and to their very limited decision-making opportunities. Oren, a soldier from the engineering corps, illustrates this in short and simple terms: 'You don't have so much freedom to choose what you do, you have orders and you do that, after maybe you think whether it's good or not. It doesn't matter if you agree or not'.

For Shmuel, it is also clear-cut: the job of a soldier is to trust his superiors and not to deliberate about operations. While talking about an arrest operation that he had carried out as a soldier in the Givati Brigade, he explained that the job of a soldier is basically to execute orders:

> We wanted to know, it wasn't like we really didn't know why we are doing this, we know what this guy did, and why we have to take him outside on this night, we didn't get too much inside it ... we knew that if they say we have to do it, it comes from above and probably they know what they are doing. It's not our task to say 'no, we won't do it'.

Following orders, then, is one of the aspects of the 'lay' (but professionally coloured) or work-related discourse that Israeli soldiers use. We can conclude that doing their job as they are ordered to do, doing it in the best way possible, without hurting others or getting hurt themselves is very central to the way these Israeli soldiers look at their activities. Seeing their work as a job and no more than that, a job that has to be done with no questions asked, makes their position regarding the implications of the work more distant. Such strategies, then, entail implicatory denial (Cohen 2001), the displacement of responsibility, euphemistic labelling and an inhibitive form of moral agency (Bandura 2002).

Strategic Talk

After looking at professionalism from the layman's perspective that soldiers have, it is time to look at a more strategic discourse that they make use of, one that is, however, mostly used by their commanders. With this strategic discourse I would like to highlight a manner of speech that focuses on explaining, in military terms, why certain actions are carried out or why specific behaviour is necessary. Moral explanations and justifications are lifted from more personal accounts to a strategic level.

A System's Point of View

The discourse discussed here is, thus, more system-like and is, as such, different from the 'lay' discourse. In this first example this becomes clear:

> The fear we, as commanders, try to create is a fear of being caught. At this checkpoint we catch you ... if you are suspect you will be checked, you will be caught if you are suspect. Not a fear of violence, or shouting. We want order at the checkpoint, because order is professionalism.

Staying within the realm of professionalism, Adam explains here what soldiers themselves often called a 'system's point of view' or *mabat ma'arechti*. The main objective of his checkpoint is that terrorists should fear going through it because its security procedures are so thorough. Importantly, order has to be maintained at the checkpoint, as this is crucial for working professionally. This point, however, can also be used as a moral justification for activities that may harm others. Soldiers or commanders use a system's point of view like this to indicate how they speak as part of the system.

In the next quote, this point of view is clearly visible. Eviatar, a former company commander of an elite unit of the artillery, explains a mission from a completely different viewpoint than that of a soldier. He does not only look at one checkpoint to see how it functions, but includes the security of the whole section in his analysis of the situation. His point of view is, then, much broader than that of normal soldiers and, because of his function, more responsibility is taken by him:

> The goal of your mission is not to stop the 3 cars you are supposed to stop, but it is to form a security force that checks, that reacts, that forms a broader aspect of security in the section let's call it that. That's my task to explain how things should happen, what actually happens on the ground, for that you have your commanders. They understand the general spirit [*ruah*] of what really happens, how many cars go through, that's what the commanders are for.

This point of view is also expressed when commanders voice their ideas about how soldiers should function and what lessons they want to teach them. Golan, who was quoted earlier, explains how he would educate his soldiers to treat people with respect while doing their job at the same time, something he hopes that his soldiers will internalize:

> First of all that they understand the sensitivity of every word that comes out of their mouths. Like when a soldier of mine stands at a checkpoint with a gun, he has to understand, and many don't understand, they get in this mode of 'come and stop' many times you have to get into a state of mind of anger.

To communicate some kind of ... you're not a babysitter, you're a soldier, your function is not to start a conversation, you have to check the car, you can do it with a smile. Maybe the other side will think if I come here with a bomb and smile he'll let me through. So you don't have to be nice, but be respectful. It doesn't contradict. So first of all let them understand the effects of their attitude towards the local population, because if you're checking this person now, big chance you'll check him again tomorrow and the coming 4 months every morning.

In this explanation, Golan clarifies why it is so important for him to convey to his soldiers that they should do their jobs 'with a smile' and without anger; it is important to 'soften' the other side (the Palestinians) since they will come through the checkpoint again and again. Through respectful treatment one can possibly avoid friction. In what he says, two seemingly contradictory roles that a soldier should perform are mentioned: he has to be tough and do his job ('you're not a babysitter') but he should also do it with respect, maybe even with a smile on his face. This way of speaking, combining toughness and professionalism with respectful treatment, is something commanders, in particular, adopt when speaking about the important traits that their soldiers should have. Eviatar gives another good example:

I would use the terms of assertiveness [*takifut*] and politeness [*adivut*], on the face of it two opposites, but very complete from my point of view. If there is a mission and we are going to fulfil it till the end also if it means that this person has to wait here 4 hours at the checkpoint because they ask us to keep him, or if we need to check a car, we will get everything out of the car. The question is how you do it. You don't throw anything, you don't start messing in his stuff but you ask the person to take the stuff out of the car. Maybe it doesn't interest the person if you do it in a polite way, but it's more to keep our human dignity [*tselem enosh*].

The main point here is that Eviatar expects his soldiers to work professionally while refraining from harming people's property without good reason. The last sentence of Eviatar's quote is interesting: he argues that the polite behaviour of soldiers is not so much important for the Palestinians to whom it is directed as it is for the human dignity of the soldiers.

Care for the Soldiers

One of the most important issues commanders have to take into account, according to their own explanations, is the safety of their soldiers. No matter what a certain operation entails, the safety and protection of the soldiers within the force takes precedence. There seems to be a moral hierarchy: first the soldiers should be safe, then the Palestinians. The moral strategy used is a moral justification, as actions are legitimized through the use of the 'safety of the soldiers' argument.

The safety of the soldiers and the accompanying notion of self-defence are used as a way of explaining and legitimizing the potentially violent behaviour of soldiers as Tal shows:

> The first time that soldiers saw me, let's say ... take someone and push him on a couch and search him or even see me cock my weapon at someone; the first time they're in shock. I tried to explain to them all the time, don't be afraid to cock your weapon in someone's face. You don't have a choice. They are a bit afraid but every time when they are in check posts and a person would come for a discussion, immediately cock your weapon and you finish the story, if that doesn't happen then one person starts a discussion and after him another person, there is a situation, another one lets himself into the discussion, then it's a chaos, everything is to save our lives.

Tal is very straightforward here in his approach; as a commander in the Nahal 50 Battalion he made very clear that the soldiers' safety was his first priority. From his language, we can conclude that he chose a fairly aggressive approach, using a significant display of force and power to control people at the checkpoints. In his eyes, however, everything was done in order to protect the soldiers. As such, Tal legitimizes his actions by pointing to the safety of his soldiers. Guy uses the same kind of arguments. During his service as a commander he told his soldiers to behave like 'machines' when it came to their own or their comrades' safety:

> So I did tell them at the checkpoints to react, first of all, I don't mind what, but take care of yourself, if it gets to killing someone, then kill someone. And that's what happened ... There is no emotion here; I didn't have emotion in such instances. It's work, machines, it's much easier being a machine than a human being in situations like that.

This notion of taking care of one's own soldiers as a crucial aspect of the units' operations shows us an interesting professional and moral discourse, one which is directed inwards, towards the safety and well-being of the soldiers themselves.

To conclude this discussion of the professionalism theme that Israeli soldiers and commanders use, we can say that their professional discourse gives them an opportunity to distance themselves from the activities that they are involved in that may harm other human beings. Acts are normalized as 'just a job', one which has to be carried out without too much deliberation from the soldiers' side. Even when harm or suffering that is inflicted is acknowledged, the fact that one is doing one's job and trying to do it as well as possible, directs away from attributing any explicit responsibility. Activities that can potentially harm others can, furthermore, be explained away and morally justified under the name of professionalism.

Ideology

In the next section, I will group expressions of patriotism, nationalism and, for example, emotions concerning the defence of the state of Israel as ideological strategies. The cultural schemes that are invoked here to explain and justify the behaviour of soldiers are principled by nature and, hence, often involve strong convictions on the part of the soldier.

A Sense of Mission

When giving accounts of their experiences, many soldiers and commanders described a feeling that they referred to as a sense of mission, or '*shlihkut*'. This feeling was especially evoked during bigger operations, which they felt were important for the IDF and Israel as a whole. With this term, they highlighted a sense of connectedness to the nation, to the aims of the state and the military. They spoke about feeling that their presence in the OPT had a real, important justification. In Bandura's terms this is a clear moral justification in which 'pernicious conduct is made personally and socially acceptable by portraying it as serving socially worthy or moral purposes' (Bandura 2002: 103). Eviatar, who stayed in the IDF as a professional for several years after his mandatory conscription period, says the following about this feeling:

> That's the base for everything, I wouldn't have stayed in the military if ... I don't feel I was in professional service [*keva*] I just did a longer service. I'm living in a country where you have to serve 3 years and after 3 years I felt it didn't end here. That I didn't give what I wanted and could give more. I said on the day that it doesn't feel like a mission and it becomes a job, I would quit. And I did, even though the temptations were great, I got out at that point, the next phase would be a job, that wasn't a mission, that wasn't living the military.

Interestingly, and in opposition to the notions discussed before, Eviatar even states that the moment he felt his military service did not feel like a mission anymore, and started to be more like a normal job, he quit. This is to say that from the moment his service became normal and not ideological, he felt that he did not have anything to give to the IDF, referring to the republican notion of citizenship experienced in Israel. Eviatar continues by saying that he believes that every soldier who serves in the OPT does so for ideological reasons:

> Furthermore, every soldier who serves in the Territories fights for his home, that doesn't happen to an American soldier in Iraq or to a Dutch soldier of UNIFIL or so. Every soldier fights for his home. (Q: 'Do they feel it like that?') I don't believe them when they say 'I only do it because I have to' if you don't want, you don't have to serve. It's not a taboo anymore not to serve. I believe that today everyone who serves has an ideological reason, that he feels he has to do this and risk his life for it.

Dror also has a clear ideological motivation for serving and traces this back to his upbringing in a patriotic home:

> I wanted to be a pilot, I grew up in a 'militant' house. My father is very militant. There were a lot of stories about the army in the house, stories with values. (Q: 'What values?') Comradeship and brave of heart and love for the country. (Q: 'Did you feel connected to the state?') Of course, I came from there. I feel a feeling of mission, it holds you in difficult times that you know that if you don't do it and he won't then no one will. I wanted to give as much as possible. I came to the paratroopers. I wanted a military career, to be a platoon commander, but I knew if not that then at least an officer, a company commander.

Both Eviatar and Dror demonstrate a highly ideological motivated attitude towards their service. They did not join the military because they had to, but because they really wanted to and because they wanted to give whatever they could to the state. This discourse is clearly different from some of the examples given before. It is, however, important to keep in mind that such ideologically motivated ways of speaking are also, at times, used by Israeli soldiers. This can, furthermore, easily be used as a justifying or legitimizing discourse. In the next section this feeling of mission is taken a bit further in order to clarify this point.

Invoking the Security Theme: Avenging Attacks on Israel or Protecting Israeli Civilians

One notion that fits in with this ideological strategy within soldiers' discourse is the idea that attacks on Israel have to be avenged. By attacks on Israel one could be referring to terrorist attacks on buses, hotels or restaurants, for example. As seen before when Operation Defensive Shield (ODS) and the soldiers' experiences of it were discussed, such events within Israeli society can have a far-reaching impact on how soldiers in the field feel and behave. A certain 'sense of mission' was said to overcome soldiers when they associated their duty within the OPT with the attacks on Israeli civilian centres. Military activities, then, became morally justified in light of the happenings within Israel.

Suddenly the boring work at the checkpoints or the routine of arrests became more meaningful as the soldiers realized the impact their work could have; they could be stopping or arresting potential terrorists at that very moment: 'But there were people, especially with the chain of bombings, it started with Hotel Park, I don't remember there was this week of another 4–5 bombings, that's it, the IDF now has to take everything down. It's something that you felt. People said "come on let's go in, we have to" ... and all of that'.

In the above quote, Yossi, a Nahal commander who participated in operations under fire during Operation Defensive Shield, recalls the mood of the soldiers around him and the language of revenge that was present. However, not only during operations such as ODS can this rhetoric be found. Assaf recalls how soldiers in his unit of the Golani Battalion reacted to talks about morality and proper behaviour given by their superiors:

> And there were soldiers who said 'what, no way, if he has a bomb, I would beat him up completely. Tomorrow he blows up my mother in Tel Aviv' so there would be the commanders that talked about the need to keep up ethics and the purity of arms and the soldiers talked straight from their emotion and their heart.

A clear association is made by the soldiers whom Assaf is quoting between their behaviour towards Palestinian suspects or terrorists and the safety of their own families within Israeli civil society. The discrepancy between the 'official' discourse of the moral code of the IDF and the emotions of the soldiers is also touched upon; soldiers speak 'from their hearts'.

Assaf also served during ODS himself and remembers how he and his comrades felt that their work was directly linked to the security of Israel:

> It was obvious, every day there were explosions in Israel; you go to Jenin two days after we went there, there was a bomb in Megiddo. The soldiers feel it. It's really not the cliché, 'our soldiers secure the borders of the north so Kiyriat Shemona won't be bombed'[54] it was really 'pointed', if you don't chase this guy on the few hundred meters you are in charge of stopping those who run with the farmers, there will be a bomb in Megiddo, just like that.

Another example of a feeling of mission is given by Golan. When he caught one of his superiors stealing a poster from a Palestinian house during an arrest operation, he told him off. This superior became very angry and called him a 'leftist' who did not care about Israel. Golan then reacted as follows:

> So back in the base I told him, 'listen my friends are also being blown up', and I had a lot of problems ... I could leave, but I didn't want to, I felt I have to be in the Territories, because it's important, however bad it is. So I told him, 'listen I don't have to be here, I'm here because I believe that what we do is important.'

In his angry reply, Golan made clear that he served in the Territories from choice, because he really thought it was important and not because someone had sent him there randomly. He, furthermore, directly linked

---

54. Kiyriat Shemona is one of the northern cities in Israel that has often come under fire from Hezbollah forces situated in South Lebanon.

the safety of his friends at home with his work in the Territories. Interestingly, a much greater amount of responsibility is taken here by soldiers and commanders for their own actions. As, in their eyes, their activities are morally and ideologically justified, they seem to have no problem in taking responsibility, thereby legitimizing the suffering caused by their actions by means of the justified cause they are serving.

Avenging the Death of Comrades

Through a story in the media in 2005, the existence of extreme feelings (and actions) of revenge amongst Israeli soldiers became public. For the first time, members of an elite unit gave their account of a military action that took place in 2002 to avenge the death of six fellow soldiers who were shot and killed at a checkpoint by Palestinian militants. The orders they received were to shoot as many Palestinian policemen as they could. The claim made was that these policemen did not stop the militants at their checkpoints and were, hence, to blame for the soldiers' deaths. During the course of one night, fifteen policemen, most of them unarmed, were shot while they were on duty at these checkpoints. The story came out in the media a few years after the killing occurred and included a videotape of the events, edited with music by members of the unit that had been involved in the operation.[55]

This very serious and controversial story (which shocked the Israeli public and shook its ideas about the morality of its soldiers) is a good, but very extreme, example of activities based on revenge, in this case attacks on the soldiers' comrades were avenged. However, the case does involve the same ideological emotions as those involved in less extreme cases that can also trigger soldiers and their commanders to act in specified, often violent, ways.

This example also demonstrates the profound danger that such ideological strategies can entail. Certain feelings, such as those discussed above, can become justifications for illegitimate violence, harassment of the other and even actual atrocities as the 'other' indiscriminately becomes 'the enemy' who has to be dealt with. The 'other' is dehumanized (Bandura 2002) and although responsibility for any potential suffering that is inflicted during military activities is taken, this hardship is not perceived as problematic as the actions are seen as legitimate.

From the above we can understand how much ideological feelings of patriotism, a sense of mission and feelings provoking revenge attacks can influence the actions of soldiers and the way they behave towards others. The ideological theme is a strong tool for explaining activities

---

55. For reports on these events see the following newspaper articles www.washing-tonpost.com/wp-dyn/content/article/2005/06/10/AR2005061001900_pf.html as accessed on 15 July 2008, www.nytimes.com/2005/06/04/international/middleeast/04mideast.html as accessed on 15 July 2008.

as it involves emotions that are difficult for an outsider to refute, which makes them even more powerful when trying to convince others.

This is a tool that is used by soldiers; they claim that if you were not there you will not be able to understand it. This claim, which is related to issues of witnessing and the power of 'being there', is very strong indeed. However, it can be easily abused to explain away and legitimize harmful behaviour and to discard any critical voices that may be heard coming from outside.

No Need for Explanation

Up until now the themes discussed were themes that soldiers used to explain, justify and legitimize their behaviour and activities. However, as Cohen mentions in his work on denial (2001), sometimes there seems to be no need to justify or legitimize actions because the actor involved in certain behaviour that seems unjust to an outsider does not perceive it as such. If someone takes his or her actions as completely legitimate, there seems to be no need to explain. Maoz already discerned this in her research about soldiers in the First Intifada between 1987 and 1993: '[L] egitimizers tend to minimize the emotional impact of the Intifada and describe themselves as untroubled by its after-effects' (Maoz 2001: 252).

The discourse used, then, does not acknowledge any harm done to others and as such no responsibility is taken for this harm, just as if it was not there. In such cases, the behaviour of soldiers is completely normalized and no more thought is given to it. The moral strategy that is used here is what Cohen calls interpretative denial; activities and consequences are not denied, however their meaning is neutralized and not seen as problematic (Cohen 2001). Maoz calls these 'emotional mechanisms of routinization, disassociation, and distancing in coping with the violence experience of the Intifada' (Maoz 2001: 251). A good example is the following testimony collected by Breaking the Silence:

> I was guarding with a guy from the company, not one of the officers, and, he told me a story, trying to explain why he didn't consider himself among those who abuse, and why he [could think he] used force and violence only when necessary. He told me a story about a patrol he was on, and this story was an example of why he didn't use force. He was on the patrol with an officer. You know the patrols – stopping the cars, sometimes confiscating the vehicles, sometimes delaying the people. When you stop a car – when you're on patrol, when you're at a checkpoint or anywhere else – you set the rules. You have the weapon, so you set the rules. So he said to the people: 'No speaking on cellular phones.' One of the Arabs in the car was on the phone and signalled that he was just finishing up the call and would be off in a second. And the guy who was telling me the story paused, and asked me: 'Do you understand?! Do you understand that the Arab signalled with his hand and told me to wait a second?! So of course I put the gun barrel to his ribs.' That

incident took place right in front of an officer. The guy telling the story had this look of amazement in his eyes that a person, an Arab, an older person, dared to signal with his hand while talking on the phone, so he placed the gun barrel to the guy's ribs. That was the story that brought to my attention that what I used to think was out of the ordinary is actually quite ordinary.

(BS Z 2902)

Here, the person described does not see or realize the gravity of his actions. He explains why he behaves in a violent manner, thus acknowledging his actions, but sees his activities as completely legitimate. There seems to be no doubt in his mind as to the righteousness of his actions. The situation around him is so normalized that his arguments make perfect sense to him.

In the following answer given by Barak, who served as a soldier in the Golani Brigade, to the question of whether he came across situations that he did not agree with during his service, it is clear that he sees his activities during his military service as completely justified. According to him, he never saw the suffering of someone who did not deserve it, he only saw people who shot at him and who, thus, deserved the treatment they received: 'No never, I never saw anything that I thought was wrong or that gave me an inner conflict. Nothing like that happened. I just came into contact with people that shot at me. I never saw someone who I felt sorry for'.

When actions become so natural to a person to the point that no explanation or legitimization seems to be needed, dangerous situations can occur. No internal moral mechanism is triggered and unjust behaviour can be carried out easily without feelings of guilt. In Bandura's terms the moral self-sanctions we naturally have are then disengaged from our conduct, this conduct generating a purely neutral meaning in our eyes.

Critical Voices: Moral Re-sensitizing

The last kind of moral strategy that I would like to discuss is the one that contradicts many of the former themes that we have explored. It is, however, an important one as it shows us a different side of soldiers' discourse that cannot be ignored. The strategy I am referring to is that of re-sensitizing, of finding some kind of connection with the victim, of acknowledging the suffering and pain of the 'other' and of truly sympathizing with them (Lifton 1973). Maoz's 'ambivalent' soldier fits well here (2001). Whereas most soldiers quoted in this work had some reservations, the ones discussed here had clear doubts about the violence used within the OPT against Palestinians.

You could say that soldiers who use this strategy see the 'other' as a human being and as an individual. They do this, for example, by making a comparison with their own situation to realize more deeply how the other person involved in the interaction must feel.

'If it Was My Home'

Some soldiers took the step of comparing a scene that they came across, for example a Palestinian house in the middle of the night, with their own situation back home. How would they react, they ask themselves, if a few foreign soldiers suddenly barged into their home and terrified their little brother and sister? How would they react if they saw their elderly father being told to pull up his shirt and pull down his pants at a checkpoint? When such questions are asked, the soldier in question is identifying deeply with the 'other' or the victims of his actions – he puts himself in their place.

The soldiers who made such comparisons usually did so after their service was over and after they had the opportunity to reflect on their experiences in the field from a physical and mental distance. During their presence in the OPT, such reflection was almost impossible due to factors described earlier, factors such as having no time to think things through or being too tired and numbed by the workload.

Lifton calls this identification with one's victims 're-sensitization' (1973) when he explains how soldiers in situations of war, the Vietnam War in his case, with clear definitions of who was their enemy, could still feel sympathy for members of the other side. Quite a number of soldiers testified to occasionally feeling such identification. Often, however, this identification came after their discharge from the military. Assaf gives a clear example:

> It was bad, it doesn't matter, also if you checked and everything was okay and you didn't hold them up for a minute, they … it's not nice when a boy, I would always think of my father, a boy of my age would come to him, I would imagine my father and a friend of mine he didn't know, who is he to tell him to get his hands up, to put up his shirt up to his armpits and turn around, who is he that he will tell him? Where is the respect, and if he looks suspicious and I would put him on the side in front of all his children and I would check with that device and I would have someone else check him and stand in front of him with a weapon just because he grew a beard because his father just died. And I think he is suspicious and he didn't have water to wash so he is dirty … but these are things I know now because I matured and saw other things. Then … you're like 'catch terrorists, respect', that here there won't be [a terror attack].

As Little as Possible

As already discussed above, there is a notion in soldiers' discourse about doing their work without hurting anyone. This can come, as we have seen before, from an idea that such behaviour is unprofessional and doesn't 'look good' but it can, of course, also come from a genuine sense of the importance of caring for another human being. The soldiers using this discourse, then, really seem to acknowledge the suffering of the 'other' and see the person in front of them as a human being like themselves, a notion that does not always seem to come naturally to soldiers. These soldiers seem uncomfortable with their role as occupiers and stress continuously that they would curb the damage they were doing as much as possible during their service. Ben-Ari came across similar attitudes when doing research within his own reserve unit during the First Intifada in the 1990s. He conveys how he and his fellow soldiers tried to 'account for our actions in terms of somehow humanizing the occupation' (Ben-Ari 1998: 179). Doron, who makes an effort to explain his attitude towards the Palestinian population, provides a good example:

> But still, I had days at checkpoints where you have the most friction with the Palestinians, and I would say to myself a lot of times, in the end they're human beings, really, I would try, in a lot of situations, to come towards them as much as possible [*lekratam*]. Even if I would get different orders. They would say close the checkpoint, no one goes through, you don't have to give a shit and then a mother would come with 2 babies in her arms, she would say I need to go, I don't know, to the clinic, 'go through', what can I say to you. It's okay, there were a lot of instances I would look the other way and I would come towards them but there were a lot of instances that I would know they were trying to play with that, and then on purpose I wouldn't let them, I would radicalize my opinions, and my stances and I wouldn't let them play with it. In general I would come towards them a lot. Usually I saw them as human beings and only 5 percent of them as terrorists, all the rest are really people that want to live quietly.

Yossi explains how important it was for him, coming from a leftist *kibbutz* background, to treat every human being as such, no matter if he was a terrorist or not:

> And one of the first things that is written in the ethical code of the IDF, is human dignity and comradeship. And I think that on the subject of the checkpoints, it was a subject that was obliged also for me, also for the soldiers and for everyone actually, to show this ... It's something that ... for me it was easier to respect this and to do this because of the education from home, the leftist thing, to give them a state, and ... to give them a chance and this and that, this helped me in the end, because I, from the beginning and also after Jenin and all that, I think I had not the intelligence identification, it is possible I checked terrorists and possible I didn't, but to give them all respect at the checkpoints, if they are women if there isn't a female police officer then don't check and only check men, and to check with respect, don't take the vehicles apart.

Yossi emphasizes in this example that, especially after the heavy fighting in the refugee camp of Jenin during Operation Defensive Shield, many soldiers had difficulties treating Palestinians respectfully because of feelings of revenge and because of anger about the attacks in Israel and the loss of the lives of soldiers that the IDF had to cope with.

A few interviewees had even more 'deviant' or critical ideas than most; they were different because of their highly critical outlook on the military and its activities in the OPT. These soldiers generally came from a leftist upbringing and seemed to sympathize with the Palestinians who suffered from the activities of the IDF more than others.

However, as these soldiers were still acting within the same military framework that they were criticizing, they felt that they did not have a lot of opportunities to act upon their critical thoughts. Gal, who is now active within the organization Breaking the Silence and who served in Battalion 50 of the Nahal Brigade, sums up the emotions he felt during his service as follows: 'So there was this thought that okay we will do it, we will get through it, we will do it as good as possible, we'll harm as little as possible, we will get through it, it will be okay'.

He and his comrades were some of the first soldiers during the Second Intifada who felt that they had to take action, to 'do something' against the situation that they were encountering in the OPT, especially in Hebron. They decided not to make too much noise outside of the military, however, trying instead to promote change from within, without involving the public or the press. Within their unit they published articles that were critical of the situation and asked questions about the reasons they had to be in the OPT. A clear moral outlook was present here. This, however, did not result in concrete activities that could really change the reality these soldiers found themselves in.

In a critical tone, Doron explained how the military trusts its soldiers to be moral without clearly getting across what their behaviour should be. The soldiers are left in a moral vacuum within which they have to cope as well as they can:

> That's a thing, that I believe that the military doesn't put enough thought in, they trust that people will be moral ... so okay the child is a wanted man, but in the house there are 8 other brothers, parents, two grandmothers and four uncles. How you treat them? Me and my friends, usually like normal human beings, you know that they usually haven't done anything; you treat them the best you can. That's it.

Such moral considerations taken into account by soldiers are important to point out. The moral agency that is shown here is again of an inhibitive nature; it entails refraining from inhumane behaviour (Bandura 2002). The actual realization that certain activities are immoral or illegitimate, however, often comes late or leaves the soldier in an isolated position with not much room to act upon it.

Conclusion

In this chapter several dominant discursive strategies used by Israeli soldiers when giving accounts of their experiences were discussed. Strategies of passivity, professionalism and ideology were used in some way or another to explain, justify and legitimize actions and decision making in the field. While most strategies involved acknowledgement of the suffering of the 'other', in certain instances the victims of actions carried out by soldiers were not recognized as such. Moral strategies that were uncovered showed aspects of moral disengagement, such as moral justification, euphemistic labelling, advantageous comparison and displacement of responsibility (Bandura 2002). Furthermore, two of the types of denial distinguished by Cohen were also found: implicatory and interpretative denial.

In most cases soldiers realized that their activities and presence within the OPT caused harm to Palestinian civilians. This realization, however, almost never spurred the soldiers into action to change the situation they and the Palestinians were in. A sense of acceptance of the existing situation was very persistent and soldiers seemed to not be motivated or willing to change it.

Responsibility for the soldiers' activities and the potential harm it could cause was, then, through the use of several strategies, avoided at all times. A passive, professional or idealist discourse helped the soldiers and their commanders to distance themselves from the consequences of their actions, partly neutralizing these.

After having looked at the spaces soldiers work in, the operational dynamics of their tasks and their discourse, I believe to have gotten closer to a deeper understanding of Israeli soldiers' behaviour and their moral outlook on their reality. In the next and final chapter, I will conclude my argument and also show how I think this work can be used within other contexts.

CHAPTER 8

CONCLUSION

My main goal with this work was to gain a deeper understanding of the everyday experiences and the moral behaviour and decision making of Israeli soldiers engaged in the practice of occupation in the Palestinian Territories. This understanding I was looking for would go beyond the most common strategy of politicians and military officials: simply seeing soldiers' aggressive and harassing behaviour as immoral 'anomalies' and leaving it at that. Too many factors seemed at play to reach this conclusion and it was, therefore, my goal to investigate these factors in detail. I have tried to show the reader the manifold facets at work when soldiers engage in military operations in asymmetrical conflict or occupation. Because of the specific nature of their activities, which can be seen as principally constabulary actions, soldiers find themselves in situations within which their senses are numbed, their stress levels rise and their moral abilities become compromised.

I have argued, by giving detailed descriptions of the arenas these soldiers work within and the operational dynamics that are part and parcel of them, that the spatial aspects of soldiers' work has a profound influence on their moralities; their behaviour and the way they view the 'other'. I have, furthermore, reasoned that within these spaces soldiers construct a discourse that legitimizes, denies and/or explains their often violent behaviour. These discourses are produced by the soldiers within the context of soldiering under occupation in spaces they often control, but that also influence their reasoning and behaviour at the same time.

Instances of misbehaviour of Israeli soldiers are then not isolated incidents as many commentators are quick to state when they (accidentally) find their way to the press. I strongly believe that the discourse of 'rotten apples' is used in order to help the IDF to keep up its moral image of itself and the Israeli state as a whole to save its image that is being attacked more and more by the international world. My study has found that the work of soldiers and its spatial and situational factors, which are the direct product of Israeli political and military policies of occupation, is for a great part responsible for the use of violence by soldiers, their disrespect to Palestinians and often harassing behaviour. This behaviour is then of a structural, systemic kind, that should be viewed in the light of the situational context it takes place in.

Thus, I argue that we should look, in the Israeli context and also outside of it, from a more structural perspective at the circumstances soldiers are placed in during such conflicts and also criticize their presence in these situations and surroundings. Taking this presence (the occupation) as a given does not suffice here. One should critically investigate and reassess its necessity.

The Systemic Approach: Taking the Israeli Case Outside of its Borders

Because of the structural characteristics of the Israeli case, it can be of help when looking at other, similar conflicts elsewhere in order to make sense of soldiers' behaviour. I believe that, specific as the Israeli case may be, it can also teach us about other instances of asymmetrical conflict in other contexts. Not only do American or Dutch soldiers, for example, find themselves in morally ambiguous situations in places such as Afghanistan and Iraq, they are also, just like Israeli soldiers, part of a more structural process in which the immoral behaviour of soldiers is made possible by the situational and spatial circumstances they find themselves in.

I do realize that there are differences between the Israeli case and the cases of other militaries involved in asymmetrical conflict. First of all, Israeli soldiers fight 'close to home' and are ideologically closer to the objectives of their military mission as this directly involves their own country. American or Dutch soldiers serving in Iraq or Afghanistan will, I expect, have fewer ideological ideas concerning their service in those countries or will at least be less personally involved with the aims of these operations. However, as I have shown, when in the field Israeli soldiers also do not have many ideological aspirations and instead busy themselves with their daily activities. All soldiers, Israeli or of other nationalities, become much more involved when it comes to the safety of their comrades than when they are confronted with issues on a state level.

A second difference between Israeli and other soldiers is the fact that Israeli soldiers are conscripts, while most soldiers of other nationalities are part of a professional army. However, from material written by US soldiers in Iraq, for example (see, for example, Buzzell 2005; Hartley 2006), it seems that the experiences of soldiers in the field and emotions that arise are very similar. Israeli and American or Dutch soldiers alike find themselves at checkpoints or on patrols for hours or days at a time, they have to conquer the heat and the cold, and they have to engage in contact with a population that is often not very sympathetic to their presence. They are afraid for their own and their comrades' safety and they feel numbed and frustrated.

If we look at the similarities between the Israeli case and other national contexts, we see that the type of tasks that have to be performed by either Israeli or Dutch or American soldiers are very similar. All have to perform constabulary tasks during which they increasingly come into contact with civilians. Such tasks involve the patrolling of cities, villages and roads, the performance of nightly arrests and the manning of checkpoints.

These tasks are all part of the practices of occupation, may this be in the OPT, Iraq or Afghanistan. Such practices characterize a policy designed to control the movements of another people through checking identity papers and setting up roadblocks, for example. Not only the complexity of the tasks and the situation on the ground are comparable, the processes of power that are present in all cases are also similar. Young, armed soldiers stand in front of civilians who are culturally very different from them and over whom they have a lot of control. The threat of attacks from out of the midst of these civilians is always present, leading to the appearance of the emotions of fear and frustration on the part of the soldiers.

These similar circumstances lead to similar behaviour on the part of the soldiers and to a similar effect on their moral professionalism. Soldiers face emotional, physical and cognitive challenges that are very much comparable. I am, therefore, convinced that we can learn from the Israeli case when looking at other, asymmetrical conflicts in which other militaries are involved.

Space and its Dynamics

I propose to look at other, similar cases and first of all look at space. Just as I did in the Israeli case, it would be very worthwhile if more research would be done on the spaces in which soldiers work. Zimbardo gives a good example with his detailed description of the Abu-Ghraib prison (2007: 332–37); he emphasizes the history of the building, its tower that is the main target for many militants in the surrounding areas and the fact that there was no sewage system and no mess halls; soldiers had to eat out of containers. Such circumstances that belong to a specific space and its dynamics are crucial to take into account, as Zimbardo does, when we want to understand the horrors that take place within this space.

Second, we should closely look at the operational dynamics within the spaces soldiers work in. Issues such as power relations between soldiers themselves, between soldiers and commanders and between soldiers and 'the enemy' or civilians should be investigated. Furthermore boredom and routine faced by the soldiers should be taken seriously as a influencing aspect of their behaviour. As my study has shown, these dynamics profoundly shape soldiers' behaviour.

In order to do so, the discourse of soldiers should be taken into account. Taking their words, concepts and interests seriously, as I have tried to do in this study, opens a world of opportunity to understand their experiences from their point of view and thus take seriously their worries or strategies of legitimating or denial, such as I found time and again. Analyzing their discourse, then, while taking into account their spatial surroundings can bring us to a meaningful understanding of their moralities and behaviour.

I'm convinced that by looking at the abovementioned issues, soldiers' (mis)behaviour within other instances of asymmetrical conflict or occupation can be better understood and perhaps prevented. It can, furthermore, help to contradict the damaging discourses of 'anomalies' or rotten apples, which take neither the situation of the soldiers seriously nor the reality of the situation on the ground for the civilian population.

Taking Responsibility

When we speak about the necessity to take a more structural or systemic approach when looking at the misconduct of soldiers, the issue of collective moral responsibility appears, which takes us beyond the picture of the lone soldier as 'rotten apple'. This work has tried to show how space and its circumstances, such as cold, heat, fear, stress and frustration, can numb soldiers' bodies and minds and, with that, their moral competency. Placing soldiers in such conditioning circumstances is not the result of a lack of choice but is, rather, a conscious decision made by policymakers at the level of the state. The question of responsibility then arises. I adhere to an approach that looks beyond the individual responsibility of soldiers and which takes into consideration other factors that bring soldiers into the situations they find themselves in, especially in the Israeli case of compulsory conscription, without losing individual responsibility from sight.

Crawford (2007) has looked into the issue of atrocities carried out by soldiers and the question of responsibility taken for it. She speaks about 'systemic atrocity' when, for instance, actions taken by soldiers result in many civilian victims. 'Systemic' here refers to the fact that responsibility for the deaths of innocents should be seen in light of a bigger system, which has placed the soldiers in a situation that made such (often illegal, but sometimes calculated) behaviour possible. This situation can, furthermore, hamper the moral competence of soldiers and thus responsibility should not only be allocated to them or their direct commanders. Crawford separates three different levels of collective responsibility besides the individual responsibility of the soldiers themselves. The first level she distinguishes as the organizational level within which military organizations can be grouped; then there is a collective moral responsibility on a state level; and finally we can find collective moral responsibility on the political and public level. Responsibility for the acts of soldiers can, then, depending on its specifics, be attributed to several different parties, while not losing from sight the fact that soldiers are moral agents themselves and should be able to distinguish right from wrong at a basic level.

Crawford thus claims that responsibility for violent acts committed by soldiers should not only be sought at the individual level of the soldiers. Because 'war is a social activity [and] not the result of uncoordinated acts of isolated individuals' (Crawford 2007: 196), responsibility for acts within war should be looked for from several different parties, such as the military, the state and also the public that supports the policymakers who decide to go to war.

As stated before, Crawford also shows that the moral capabilities of soldiers are often compromised by the situation they are put in by the military and the state. While I have shown in this study that the circumstances soldiers find themselves in produce processes of numbing and affect the moral competence of soldiers, Crawford emphasizes the external factors that put soldiers in these circumstances in the first place.

In an article on the massacre of civilians by American soldiers in Haditha, Iraq, Lifton calls the situations soldiers are put in within such conflict 'atrocity-producing situations' (2006). He writes: 'To be sure, individual soldiers and civilians who participated in it are accountable for their behaviour, even under such pressured conditions. But the greater responsibility lies with those who planned and executed the war in Iraq and the "war on terrorism" of which it is part' (ibid.).

Most of the instances of misconduct by Israeli soldiers encountered in this study were part of a daily form of harassment and were not full-blown atrocities such as those that Crawford and Lifton speak of. This behaviour, which often is not categorized as war crimes or even as illegitimate or illegal activity, should, however, be looked at as it paves the road for more serious abuses of power. The everyday nature of this behaviour, furthermore, makes it 'normal' and almost 'invisible'; thus, when a more serious act or an atrocity takes place, it becomes easier to determine the latter as such, the daily acts of misbehaviour simply being ignored as irrelevant in comparison. For minor acts this is a cloudy issue; many actions are seen as legitimate and are condoned by commanders and thus soldiers do not have the sense that they are doing 'something wrong'. Their moral awareness can become blurred or numbed by the situation that they are in and because of the normalization of harassing or violent acts, which are not understood as such and for which no responsibility is therefore taken. I thus believe that this behaviour should be taken seriously as well, and should also be seen in the light of a systemic approach with regard to who is responsible for it.

Both Crawford's and Lifton's ideas, then, support my claim that in the Israeli case, but certainly also in other contexts, we are in dire need of a broader, outward vision when trying to understand and possibly prevent the misconduct by soldiers. We should start by avoiding 'putting people in situations where they are more likely to commit atrocities' (Crawford 2007: 197). Militaries should, furthermore, also look further than the ethical training of soldiers or the jailing of individual soldiers as 'extreme' cases and see the problems that their soldiers face within a wider context and as a structural problem. Moral agency, it should be recognized, has structural features that we should seriously consider (ibid.: 211).

If no responsibility is taken for the 'atrocity-producing' situation that soldiers find themselves in, the harassing and illegal behaviour of soldiers will never come to an end. Without legitimizing such behaviour, we should look closely at the factors at play when (moral) behaviour is shaped and then subsequently take a step back to look at the forces and structures that are really responsible.

REFERENCES

Amireh, A. 2003. 'Between Complicity and Subversion: Body Politics in Palestinian National Narrative', *The South Atlantic Quarterly* 102(4): 747–72.

Andoni, G. 2001. 'A Comparative Study of *Intifada* 1987 and *Intifada* 2000', in R. Carey (ed), *The New Intifada: Resisting Israel's Apartheid*. London: Verso.

Arendt, H. 1963. *Eichmann in Jerusalem*. New York: Penguin Books.

Augé, M. 1995. *Non-Places: Introduction of an Anthropology of Supermodernity*. London: Verso.

Baarda, van T. and D. Verweij 2006. 'Military Ethics: Its Nature and Pedagogy', in T. van Baarda and D. Verweij (eds.), *Military Ethics the Dutch Approach: a Practical Guide*. Leiden: Martinus Nijhoff Publishers.

Bandura, A. 1991. 'Social Cognitive Theory of Moral Thought and Action', in W.M. Kurtines and J.L. Gewirtz (eds.), *Handbook of Moral Behavior and Development*. Hillsdale, NJ: Erlbaum.

Bandura, A. 1999. 'Moral Disengagement in the Perpetration of Inhumanities', *Personality and Social Psychology Review* 3(3): 193–209.

Bandura, A. 2002. 'Selective Moral Disengagement in the Exercise of Moral Agency', *Journal of Moral Education* 31(2): 101–19.

Bar-Tal, D. 1990. 'Causes and Consequences of Delegitimization: Models of Conflict and Ethnocentrism', *Journal of Social Issues* 46(1): 65–81.

Bauman, Z. 1989. *Modernity and the Holocaust*. Oxford: Polity Press.

Baumann G. and A. Gingrich. 2006. *Grammars of Identity/Alterity: A Structural Approach*. New York: Berghahn Books.

Ben-Amos, A. and I. Bet-El. 1999. 'Holocaust Day and Memorial Day in Israeli Schools: Ceremonies, Education and History', *Israel Studies* 4(1): 258–84.

Ben-Ari, E. 1998. *Mastering Soldiers: Conflict, Emotions and the Enemy in an Israeli Military Unit*. New York: Berghahn Books.

Ben-Ari, E. 2008. 'Between Violence and Restraint: Human Rights, Humanitarian Considerations, and the Israeli Military in the Al-Aqsa *Intifada*', in T. van Baarda and D. Verweij (eds.), *The Moral Dimension of Asymmetrical Warfare: Counter-Terrorism, Western Values and Military Ethics*. Leiden: Martinus Nijhoff Publishers.

Ben-Ari, E, Z. Lerer, U. Ben-Shalom and A. Vainer. 2010. *Rethinking Contemporary Warfare: a Sociological View of the Al-Aqsa Intifada*.

New York: State University of New York.

Ben-Ari, E, D. Maman and Z. Rosenhek. 2000. 'Military Sociological Research in Israel', in G. Kummel and A. Prufort (eds.), *Military Sociology: The Richness of a Discipline*. Baden-Baden: Nomos Publishers.

Ben-Ari, E., M. Maymon, N. Gazit and R. Shatzberg. 2004. *From Checkpoints to Flow-points: Sites of Friction between the Israel Defence Forces and Palestinians*. Jerusalem: Harry S. Truman Institute of the Advancement of Peace, the Hebrew University.

Ben-Shalom, U., Z. Lehrer and E. Ben-Ari. 2005. 'Cohesion during Military Operations: A Field Study on Combat Units in the Al-Aqsa *Intifada*', *Armed Forces and Society* 32(1): 63–79.

Besteman, C. 1996. 'Representing Violence and Othering in Somalia', *Cultural Anthropology* 11(1): 120–33.

Browning, C. 1992. *Ordinary Men: Reserve Police Battalion 101 and the Final Solution in Poland*. New York: HarperCollins Publishers, Inc.

Buzzell, C. 2005. *My War: Killing Time in Iraq*. New York: G.P. Putnam's Sons.

Cohen, S. 2001. *States of Denial: Knowing about Atrocities and Suffering*. Oxford: Blackwell Publishers Inc.

Cohen, T., R. Montoya and C. Insko. 2006. 'Group Morality and Intergroup Relations: Cross-Cultural and Experimental Evidence', *Personality and Social Psychology Bulletin* 32(11): 1559–72.

Crawford, N. 2007. 'Individual and Collective Moral Responsibility for Systemic Military Atrocity', *The Journal of Political Philosophy* 15(2): 187–212.

Creveld, van M. 1998. *The Sword and the Olive: A Critical History of the Israeli Defense Forces*. New York: Public Affairs.

Dar, Y. and S. Kimhi. 2001. 'Military Service and Self-Perceived Maturation Among Israeli Youth', *Journal of Youth and Adolescence* 30(4): 427–48.

Dar, Y., S. Kimhi, N. Stadler and A. Epstein. 2000. 'The Imprint of the *Intifada*: Response of Kibbutz-Born Soldiers to Military Service in the West Bank and Gaza', *Armed Forces and Society* 26(2): 285–311.

Dekker, M. 2011. 'Building a Nation under Occupation: Fragmented Sovereignty, Security Sector Reform, and the Issue of Legitimacy in the Context of Occupation', *Etnofoor* 23(2): 37–56.

Douglas, M. 2002 [1966] *Purity and Danger: an Analysis of the Concepts of Pollution and Taboo*. London: Routledge Classics.

Doumani, B. 2004. 'Scenes from Daily Life: the View from Nablus', *Journal of Palestine Studies* 34(1): 37–50.

Edel, M. and A. Edel. 1959. *Anthropology and Ethics*. Springfield: Charles C. Thomas.

Falah, G. 2005. 'The Geopolitics of "Enclavisation" and the Demise of a Two-state Solution to the Israeli–Palestinian Conflict', *Third World*

Quarterly 26(8): 1341–1372.

Foucault, M. 1995[1978]. *Discipline and Punish: the Birth of the Prison.* New York: Vintage Books.

Franke, V. 1999. 'Resolving Identity Tensions: The Case of the Peacekeeper', *The Journal of Conflict Studies* 19(2): 124–143, retrieved on 21 July 2008 from http://journals.hil.unb.ca/index.php/JCS/article/view/4359/5018.

Furman, M. 1999. 'Army and War: Collective Narratives of Early Childhood in Contemporary Israel', in E. Lomsky-Feder and E. Ben-Ari (eds), *The Military and Militarism in Israeli Society.* Albany: State University of New York Press.

Furnham, A. 1988. *Lay Theories: Everyday Understanding of Problems in the Social Sciences.* Oxford: Pergamon Press.

Gazit, N. 2009. 'Social Agency, Spatial Practices, and Power: The Micro-foundations of Fragmented Sovereignty in the Occupied Territories', *International Journal of Politics, Culture and Society* 22(1): 83–103.

Goldhagen, D.J. 1996. *Hitler's Willing Executioners: Ordinary Germans and the Holocaust.* New York: Alfred A. Knopf.

Gordon, N. 2008. *Israel's Occupation.* Berkeley: University of California Press.

Graham, S., ed. 2004. *Cities, War, and Terrorism: Towards an Urban Geopolitics.* Malden: Blackwell Publishing.

Gregory, D. 2004. *The Colonial Present.* Malden: Blackwell Publishing.

Grossman, D. 1988. *Yellow Wind.* New York: Farrar, Straus and Giroux.

Grossman, D. 1995. *On Killing: the Psychological Cost of Learning to Kill in War and Society.* New York: Back Bay Books/Little, Brown and Company.

Hammami, R. 2006. *Human Agency at the Frontiers of Global Inequality: An Ethnography of Hope in Extreme Places.* Inauguration speech for the Prince Claus Chair in Development and Equity, University of Utrecht.

Hammami, R. and S. Tamari. 2001. 'The Second Uprising: End or New Beginning?', *Journal of Palestine Studies* 30(2): 5–25.

Hartley, J. 2006. *Just Another Soldier.* New York: Harper Collins Publishers.

Helman, S. 1993. *Conscientious Objection to Military Service as an Attempt to Redefine the Content of Citizenship.* PhD thesis, Department of Sociology and Anthropology, The Hebrew University of Jerusalem.

Helman, S. 1997. 'Militarism and the Construction of Community', *Journal of Political and Military Sociology* 25(Winter): 305–32.

Herbert, S. 1997. *Policing Space: Territoriality and the Los Angeles Police Department.* Minneapolis: University of Minnesota Press.

Herzog, H. 1998. 'Homefront and Battlefront: The Status of Jewish and Palestinian Women in Israel', *Israel Studies* 3(1): 61–84.

Howell, S., ed. 1997. *The Ethnography of Moralities.* London: Routledge.

Hughes, E. 1958. *Men and Their Work*. Glencoe: Free Press.

Ignatieff, M. 2001. 'Handcuffing the military? Military Judgment, Rules of Engagement and Public Scrutiny', in P. Mileham and L. Willett (eds.) *Military Ethics for the Expeditionary Era*. London: Royal Institute of International Affairs.

Izraeli, D. 2004. 'Gendering Military Service in the Israeli Defence Forces', in M. Semyonov and N. Lewin-Epstein (eds.), *Stratification in Israel: Class, Ethnicity, and Gender*. Edison: Transaction Publishers.

Kaldor, M. 2006. *New and Old Wars: Organized Violence in a Global Era*. Cambridge: Polity Press.

Kasher, A. and A. Yadlin. 2005. 'Military Ethics of Fighting Terror: An Israeli Perspective', *Journal of Military Ethics* 4(1): 3–32.

Kelman, H. and L. Hamilton. 1989. *Crimes of Obedience: Towards a Social Psychology of Authority and Responsibility*. New Haven, CT: Yale University Press.

Kimmerling, B. 1993. 'Patterns of Militarism in Israel', *European Journal of Sociology* 34(2): 196–223.

Kobrick, J. and R. Johnson. 1991. 'Effects of Hot and Cold Environments on Military Performance', in R. Gal and A. Mangelsdorff (eds.), *Handbook of Military Psychology*. Hoboken, NJ: John Wiley & Sons Ltd.

Kohlberg, L. 1969. 'Stage and Sequence: The Cognitive–Developmental Approach to Socialization', in D. Golsin (ed.), *Handbook of Socialization Theory and Research*. Chicago: Rand McNally.

Kohlberg, L. 1981. *The Philosophy of Moral Development*. Cambridge: Harper and Row.

Kohlberg, L. 1984. *The Psychology of Moral Development: The Nature and Validity of Moral Stages*. New York: Harper and Row.

Leavitt, J. 1996. 'Meaning and Feeling in the Anthropology of Emotions', *American Ethnologist* 23(3): 514–39.

Lefebvre, H. 2007 [1991]. *The Production of Space*. Oxford: Blackwell Publishers.

Levy, Y. 2003. 'Social Convertibility and Militarism: Evaluation of the Development of Military–Society Relations in Israel in the Early 2000s', *Journal of Political and Military Sociology* 31(1): 71–96.

Levy, Y. 2006. 'The War of the Peripheries: A Social Mapping of IDF Casualties in the Al-Aqsa *Intifada*', *Social Identities* 12(3): 309–24.

Levy, Y. 2007. 'Soldiers as Laborers: a Theoretical Model', *Theory and Society* 36(2): 187–208.

Levy, Y. 2008. 'The Linkage Between Israel's Military Policies and the Military's Social Composition: the Case of the Al-Aqsa *Intifada*', *American Behavioral Scientist* 51(1): 1575–1589.

Levy, Y. and S. Mizrahi. 2008. 'Alternative Politics and the Transformation of Society Military Relations: the Israeli Experience', *Administration*

& Society 40(1): 25–53.

Liebes, T. and S. Blum-Kulka. 1994. 'Managing a Moral Dilemma: Israeli Soldiers in the *Intifada*', *Armed Forces and Society* 21(1): 45–68.

Lieblich, A. 1989. *Transition to Adulthood Military Service: The Israeli Case*. Albany: State University of New York Press.

Lieblich, A. and M. Perlow. 1988. 'Transition to Adulthood during Military Service', *The Jerusalem Quarterly* 47: 40–76.

Lifton, R. 1973. *Home from the War*. New York: Touchstone Books.

Lifton, R. 2006. 'Haditha Massacre: in an "Atrocity-Producing Situation" Who is to Blame?', *Editor & Publisher*, 4 June.

Lind, W., K. Nightengale, J. Schmitt, J. Sutton, and G. Wilson. 1989. 'The Changing Face of War: Into the Fourth Generation', *Marine Corps Gazette*, October: 22–26.

Linn, R. 1996. 'When the Individual Soldier Says "No" to War: A Look at Selective Refusal during the Intifada', *Journal of Peace Research* 33(4): 421–431.

Lomsky-Feder, E. 1998. *As if There Was No War: The Life Stories of Israeli Men*. Jerusalem: Magnes Press.

Lomsky-Feder and E. Ben-Ari, eds. 1999. *The Military and Militarism in Israeli society*. Albany: State University of New York Press.

Lomsky-Feder and E. Ben-Ari, 2007. 'Identity, Politics and the Military in Contemporary Israel', manuscript, Hebrew University, Jerusalem.

Maoz, I. 2001. 'The Violent Asymmetrical Encounter with the Other in an Army–Civilian Clash: The Case of the *Intifada*', *Peace and Conflict: Journal of Peace Psychology* 7(3): 243–63.

Marshall, S.L.A. 1947. *Men Against Fire*. New York: William Morrow Press.

Marton, R. 2008. *Israel Mainstream Beliefs*, presented at the 'Jerusalem Seminar', October, The Hague (unpublished).

Mauss, M. 1979. 'The Notion of Body Techniques', *Sociology and Psychology: Essays*. London: Routledge Kegan Paul.

Mendelson-Maoz, A. 2005. 'Checkpoint Syndrome: Violence, Madness and Ethics in the Hebrew Literature of the *Intifada*', in A. Fahraeus and A. Jonsson (eds.), *Textual Ethos Studies or Locating Ethics*. Amsterdam: Rodopi.

Miller, L. and C. Moskos. 1995. 'Humanitarians or Warriors?: Race, Gender, and Combat Status in Operation Restore Hope', *Armed Forces and Society* 21(4): 613–37.

Minow, M. 2007. 'Living up to Rules: Holding Soldiers Responsible for Abusive Conduct and the Dilemma of the Superior Orders Defence', 52 *McGill L.J.*: 1–54.

Monaghan, L. 2000. 'Hard Men, Shop Boys and Others: Embodying Competence in a Masculinist Occupation', *Working Papers Series*, School of Social Sciences, Cardiff University.

Ohana, D. 1995. 'Zarathustra in Jerusalem: Nietzsche and the "New

Hebrews"', *Israeli Affairs* 1(3): 38–60.

Opotow, S. 1990. 'Moral Exclusion and Injustice: An Introduction', *Journal of Social Issues* 46 (1): 1–20.

Pressman, J. 2003. 'The Second *Intifada*: Background and Causes of the Israeli-Palestinian Conflict', *Journal of Conflict Studies* 23(2): 114–41.

Rabinowitz, D. 2001. 'Natives with Jackets and Degrees. Othering, Objectification and the Role of Palestinians in the Co-existence Field in Israel', *Social Anthropology* 9(1): 65–80.

Razack, S. 2000. 'From the "Clean Snows of Petawawa": The Violence of Canadian Peacekeepers in Somalia', *Cultural Anthropology* 15(1):127–163.

Richardson, R., D. Verweij and D. Winslow. 2004. 'Moral Fitness for Peace Operations', *Journal of Political and Military Sociology* 32(1): 99–113.

Ron, J. 2003. *Frontiers and Ghettos: State Violence in Serbia and Israel*. Berkeley: University of California Press.

Ron-Furer, L. 2003. *Checkpoint Syndrome*, retrieved on 19 June 2008 from http://www.ifamericansknew.org/download/checkpoint_syndro me.pdf.

Sacks, R. 1986. *Human Territoriality: Its Theory and History*. Cambridge: Cambridge University Press.

Sandler, S. 2003. 'War Resistance in Israel – an Overview', *The Broken Rifle* 58, retrieved on 23 January 2009 from www.wri-irg.org/ node/2481.

Seu, B. 2003. '"Your Stomach Makes You Feel That You Don't Want to Know Anything about It": Desensitization, Defence Mechanisms and Rhetoric in Response to Human Rights Abuses', *Journal of Human Rights* 2(2): 183–96.

Shamir, B. and E. Ben-Ari. 1999. 'Leadership in an Open Army? Civilian Connections, Inter-organizational Frameworks, and Changes in Military Leadership', in J. Hunt (ed.), *Out-of-the-Box Leadership: Transforming the 21ˢᵗ Century Army and other Top-performing Organization*. Stamford: JAI Press.

Shohat, E. 1990. 'Master Narrative/Counter Readings: The Politics of Israeli Cinema', in R. Sklar and C. Musser (eds) *Resisting Images: Essays on Cinema and History*. Philadelphia: Temple University Press.

Shohat, E. 1999. 'The Invention of the Mizrahim', *Journal of Palestine Studies* 29(1): 5–20.

Smeulers, A. 2004. 'What Tranforms Ordinary People into Gross Human Rights Violators?', in S. Carey and S. Poe (eds.) *Understanding Human Rights Violations: New Systematic Studies*. Aldershot: Ashgate.

Smeulers, A. and F. Grünfeld, eds. 2011. *International Crimes and Other Gross Human Rights Violations: A Multi- And Interdisciplinary Textbook*. Leiden: Brill.

Spivak, G. 1985. 'The Rani of Sirmur: An Essay in Reading the Archives',

History and Theory 24(3): 247–72.

Staub, E. 1989. *The Roots of Evil: The Origins of Genocide and Other Group Violence.* Cambridge: Cambridge University Press.

Triandafyllidou, A. 1998. 'National Identity and the Other', *Ethnic and Racial Studies* 21(4): 593–612.

Turner, T. 1995. 'Social Body and Embodied Subjects: Bodiliness, Subjectivity, and Sociality among the Kayapo', *Cultural Anthropology* 10(2): 143–70.

Verweij, D. 2002. 'The Dark Side of Obedience: The Consequences of Hannah Arendt's Analysis of the Eichmann Case', *Professional Ethics* 19(2/4): 143–58.

Verweij, D. 2007. 'Morele Professionaliteit in de Militaire Praktijk', in J. Kole and D. de Ruyter (eds.), *Werkzame Idealen.* Assen: Van Gorcum.

Verweij, D. 2008. *Denken in Dialoog: Ethiek en de Militaire Praktijk.* Inaugural lecture, Faculty of Military Sciences, Netherlands Defence Academy.

Vetlesen, A. 2005. *Evil and Human Agency: Understanding Collective Evildoing.* Cambridge: Cambridge University Press.

Williams, S. 2007. 'Vulnerable/Dangerous Bodies? The Trials and Tribulations of Sleep', *Sociological Review* 55(s1): 142–55.

Winslow, D. 1997. *The Canadian Airborne in Somalia: a Socio-cultural Inquiry.* Ottawa: Canadian Government Publishing.

Winslow, D. 2003. *Human Security.* Inaugural lecture, Faculty of Social Sciences, VU University, Amsterdam.

Wistrich, R. 1995. 'Theodor Herzl: Zionist Icon, Myth-Maker and Social Utopian', *Israeli Affairs* 1(3): 1–37.

Zanger, A. 2005. 'Blind Space: Roadblock Movies in the Contemporary Israeli Film', *Shofar: the Interdisciplinary Journal of Jewish Studies* 24(1): 37–48.

Zigon, J. 2008. *Morality: an Anthropological Perspective.* Oxford: Berg.

Zimbardo, P. 2007. *The Lucifer Effect: Understanding How Good People Turn Evil.* New York: Random House Trade Paperbacks.

INDEX